VEGETABLES

VEGETABLES

DELICIOUS RECIPES FOR ROOTS, BULBS, SHOOTS & STEMS

MASTERCHEF WINNER 2009

MAT FOLLAS

PHOTOGRAPHY BY STEVE PAINTER

RYLAND PETERS & SMALL
LONDON • NEW YORK

Photography, Design and prop styling
Steve Painter
Editor Stephanie Milner
Production David Hearn
Art Director Leslie Harrington
Editorial Director Julia Charles
Publisher Cindy Richards

Food stylist Lucy McKelvie
Indexer Hilary Bird

First published in 2016. This revised
edition published in 2020 by
Ryland Peters & Small
20–21 Jockey's Fields
London WC1R 4BW
and
341 E 116th St
New York NY 10029

www.rylandpeters.com

10 9 8 7 6 5 4 3 2 1

Text © Mat Follas 2016, 2020
Design and photographs © Ryland Peters
& Small 2016, 2020

Printed in China

ISBN: 978-1-78879-210-3

A CIP record for this book is available
from the British Library.

US Library of Congress CIP data has been
applied for.

Notes
• Both British (Metric) and American
(Imperial plus US cups) measurements
are included in these recipes for your
convenience, however it is important
to work with one set of measurements
and not alternate between the two
within a recipe.
• All spoon measurements are level unless
otherwise specified.
• All eggs are medium (UK) or large (US),
unless specified as large, in which case
US extra-large should be used. Uncooked
or partially cooked eggs should not
be served to the very old, frail, young
children, pregnant women or those with
compromised immune systems.
• Ovens should be preheated to the
specified temperatures. See page 6 for
more information. We recommend using
an oven thermometer.
• Whenever butter is called for within
these recipes, unsalted butter should
be used.
• When a recipe calls for the grated zest
of citrus fruit, buy unwaxed fruit and wash
well before using. If you can only find
treated fruit, scrub well in warm soapy
water before using.

• To sterilize preserving jars, wash them
in hot, soapy water and rinse in boiling
water. Place in a large saucepan and
cover with hot water. With the saucepan
lid on, bring the water to a boil and
continue boiling for 15 minutes. Turn off
the heat and leave the jars in the hot
water until just before they are to be filled.
Invert the jars onto a clean dish towel to
dry. Sterilize the lids for 5 minutes, by
boiling or according to the manufacturer's
instructions. Jars should be filled and
sealed while they are still hot.
• Cheeses started with animal rennet are
not suitable for strict vegetarians so read
food labelling carefully and, if necessary,
check that the cheese you buy is made
with a non-animal (microbial) starter.
Traditional Parmesan is not vegetarian.
See page 8 for more information.

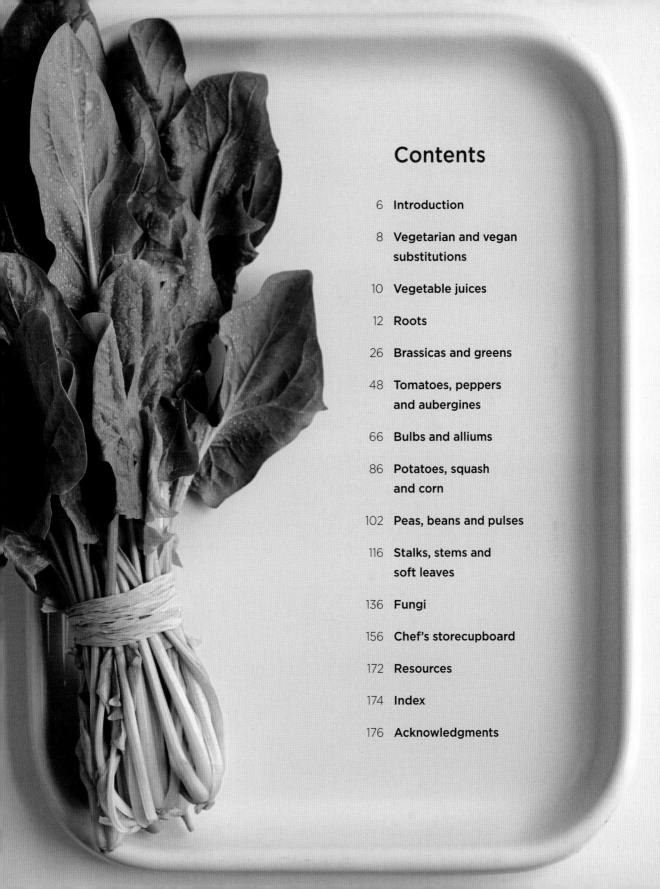

Contents

Introduction

I'm a Kiwi (New Zealander) living in the UK, for 20 years now, and I still find the English a strange bunch when it comes to eating. They always finish every plate of food, no matter how much there is on the plate, whereas I grew up with a South-east Asian influence where you always leave a little food on the plate to show your host they have served enough food. The English consider it an insult to leave anything as it implies they didn't like it. As a restaurateur and chef it's incredibly satisfying, I love that the plates are clear and there's no wastage but I personally see every clear plate as a message saying I didn't serve enough – I just can't win.

Creating vegetarian dishes is similar. I've been restricted by my upbringing and preconceptions about food. I grew up with traditional 'meat and two veg' meals. I expect to see something on a plate that is meat, to the extent that my idea was to write a cookbook of vegetable-based meals not restricted by only using vegetable products. I was thinking like a typical chef, there's a standing joke in many kitchens that any vegetarian dish can be improved with bacon, but the reality is that it shows ignorance of the options and flavours vegetables can produce.

I started cooking and testing, I realized that very few of the recipes used meat as I had initially expected them to. I could always find vegetarian alternatives that were just as good to use, if not better, and the whole process has been inspiring. For me personally it has been a journey of discovery to the amazing flavour combinations available when I have stopped being mentally limited by the requirement of a meat product on every dish. I now reach for an aubergine/eggplant, fennel bulb, some mushrooms or anything fresh from my garden for inspiration long before I reach for meat. I have written vegetarian recipes that I want to eat. Meals that I would like to eat over a meat dish. One of my bestselling dishes is the simple Red Onion Tarte Tatin with Goat's Cheese and Dandelion Sauce on page 68 – it's delicious, savoury, sweet and cheesy with hints of bitterness from the dandelions in the sauce, a perfectly balanced meal that my customers love.

A real bugbear of mine is vegetable dishes that imitate meat. I spent ages trying to make a good bean burger. What I found is that as I replaced the beans with mashed potatoes it tasted better and better, so I then tried it with no beans at all before realizing that what I had achieved was a version of one of my favourite quick lunches, a 'chip butty'. Next, I tried smoked mashed potato, something I serve in the restaurant that's hugely popular, and it got

better. I then decided to try a smoked potato rosti to get the crunch of chips – it was amazing and became the basis for The Best Burger on page 145. It's a burger on its own merits, not a meat imitation, in fact it's better. The same applies throughout the book, where I've used vegetables in place of meat like the Mushroom Toad-in-the-hole with Onion Gravy on page 146 or the Aubergine Lasagne on page 61. I've made the vegetable the star – it's not hidden or trying to imitate the flavour of meat.

With all the amazing ways we treat meat to enhance the flavour and texture, like smoking, griddling, and so on, unsurprisingly, if you apply the same processes to vegetables, they taste amazing, too. I have used many of the processes in the book, griddling the cauliflower in my Cauliflower Cheese on page 33, and smoking the tomatoes for my Smoked Tomato Ketchup on page 160.

I've written in my acknowledgments about Jo Francis, who introduced me to mushroom foraging, but there are a few other foraged ingredients used throughout the book. Try to use some of the foraged ingredients – wild garlic/ramps is my favourite example, my first restaurant was named after it, but there's also the sharpness of sorrel, the mushroomy flavour of ribwort plantain and aromatic horseradish – nothing in the animal kingdom comes close to these fresh and flavourful ingredients! Learn to forage safely from someone who knows what they are doing, don't just use a book.

My recipes are written for fan ovens, so increase the temperatures according to manufacturer's instructions if yours is conventional. Where seasoning is with salt, vinegars and chilli/chile, I suggest adding less and tasting because your palate is not the same as mine and the flavour and sweetness of vegetables will differ depending on the weather and ripeness. Most of all, enjoy trying the recipes from this book at home using fresh produce.

Vegetarian and vegan substitutions

I'm a huge cheese fan, the variety of flavours and nuances even within a single variety of cheese is vast, I would argue comparable to wine. I'm lucky enough to be a judge for The Guild of Fine Food's World Cheese Awards on a regular basis, which gives me great insight into some of the fantastic cheeses produced around the world. It is a huge shame that some cheeses, sadly Parmesan being one, are, by their definition, not vegetarian – they use animal rennet in the formation of the cheese.

There are now so many good vegetarian alternatives and most of my favourite cheeses are vegetarian. The British Cheese Awards Supreme Champion 2015 Barkham Blue is a great example of vegetarian cheese, a sublimely delicious blue cheese, sadly only produced in small volumes or I would feature it in recipes in this book.

This book is mostly vegetarian (cheeses aside) and many of the recipes are also vegan or easily modified using vegan cheeses, cream and mayonnaise. I've written recipes for my versions of these vegan basics opposite.

It is not difficult to find a vegetarian substitute for any brand or variety of cheese that isn't vegetarian. For example, in the UK, there is a fantastic hard cheese called Old Winchester that is similar in flavour and texture to a Parmesan cheese, it is also vegetarian and superior to many Parmesan cheeses in my opinion. Talk to your cheese monger at a specialist cheese shop or market cheese counter and enjoy finding some great alternatives.

My recipes list Parmesan, Cheddar, Comté and other well known varieties of cheese. A decent cheese counter will have vegetarian versions of these but, for simplicity, I have used the common names of cheeses with the appropriate flavours and textures in the recipes. You can substitute them wherever necessary.

Many ingredients also contain animal products and it's not widely known that they do. To maintain a meat-free diet, beware of many products containing anchovies especially, from tomato sauces to miso pastes or bases. The use of anchovies is very common, so check you are using a vegetarian version. Other animal products are often used in food processing or for clarifying beers and wines. Read the labels carefully before you buy these kinds of ingredients.

Dairy-free cheese

PREPARE: **5 MINUTES** COOK: **10 MINUTES (PLUS RESTING TIME OF 12 HOURS)** MAKES: **800 ML/28 OZ.**

There are many vegan cheeses about that use nuts to provide a similar texture to dairy cheese and are great to eat but they lack the flavour profile of a dairy product. This, however, is a great cheese to eat. I love it as a dip or a base for sauces and it works well used in place of dairy cheese in most recipes.

400 g/2 cups canned chopped tomatoes

300 g/2¹⁄₂ cups unroasted cashew nuts

4 teaspoons dark miso paste

50 g/3¹⁄₂ tablespoons dried onions

¹⁄₂ teaspoon table salt

50 ml/3¹⁄₂ tablespoons sherry vinegar

1 teaspoon Dijon mustard

a dash of Tabasco sauce

50 ml/3¹⁄₂ tablespoons unrefined coconut oil

Add all of the ingredients, except the coconut oil, to a saucepan, set over a low heat and bring to a low simmer. Stir to combine, then leave in the fridge overnight.

Transfer the mixture to a food processor and purée until smooth. Slowly add the coconut oil, then continue to blend until the mixture is combined and smooth.

Press the mixture into a container and chill in the fridge for at least 4 hours until firm.

Use in place of cheese for cooking, or serve on its own. It makes an amazing cheese on toast with a healthy glug of 'Shire' Sauce (page 159) on top.

Dairy-free cream

PREPARE: **2 MINUTES** COOK: **10 MINUTES** MAKES: **150 ML/5 OZ.**

I love the flavour of this cream. If you have an ice cream machine, it makes delicious ice cream with a little vanilla or some puréed fruit stirred through it. Xanthan gum is available in health food shops and larger supermarkets, usually in the gluten-free or baking section.

¹⁄₄ teaspoon xanthan gum

3 teaspoons rice flour

150 g/1¹⁄₂ cups unroasted cashew nuts, softened overnight in water

Pour 200 ml/³⁄₄ cup of water into a saucepan, set over a medium heat and bring to the boil. Pour into a food processor and start the motor.

Add the xanthan gum and rice flour, then slowly add the cashew nuts. Blend to a smooth cream.

Cool, then chill in the fridge for a few hours. Keep refrigerated for up to 4 days, or freeze in ice cube sheets for later use.

Vegetable juices

This book is about celebrating the wonderful and diverse choices for cooking with vegetables, but vegetables can also be transformed into delicious tasting, health-giving, bright coloured juices. These recipes use vegetables that are available year-round. Enjoy them at home with breakfast, on the move or as part of a picnic spread.

Kale and carrot

PREPARE: **5 MINUTES** SERVES: **4**

This juice packs a punch and is healthy and tasty! The sweet oranges and the strong iron flavour of the kale work wonderfully together.

2 large bunches of kale
200 g/7 oz. carrots, trimmed
grated zest and juice of 2 oranges

Add the kale, carrots, orange zest and the juice of 1 of the oranges to a juicer. Process until smooth, adding a little more orange juice as necessary.

Serve in tall glasses or transfer to a bottle with a screw-top lid to take out. You may need to give the juice a gentle shake before drinking.

Tomato, celery and burnt pepper

PREPARE: **10 MINUTES** SERVES: **4**

This recipe has more than a nod to a Bloody Mary cocktail. The burnt (bell) peppers give it a unique flavour and I highly recommend it with a generous glug of tequila as a pre-dinner drink.

2 red (bell) peppers
8 large tomatoes, roughly chopped
4 celery sticks, thinly sliced, plus the tops to garnish
2 tablespoons runny honey
a generous splash of smoked chipotle Tabasco sauce
freshly squeezed juice of 1/2 lemon
4 small lemon wedges, to serve

Over a naked flame, or in a very hot oven at 240°C (475°F) Gas 9, carefully blacken the outer skin of the (bell) peppers for 3–4 minutes, then brush away any loose bits of blackened skin.

Put the tomatoes, blackened peppers, celery, honey, smoked chipotle Tabasco sauce and lemon juice into a juicer and pulse to combine.

Pour the juice into glasses and serve immediately dressed with a few celery leaves and a wedge of lemon for squeezing.

Apple and beetroot

PREPARE: **10 MINUTES**
COOK: **45 MINUTES** SERVES: **2**

Beetroot/beets and apple is a wonderful combination that I often use in the restaurant as a purée or, with more apple juice like this recipe, as a delicious taster between courses. This is not an instant juice but the taste of the beetroot/beets cooked in apple juice makes it worthwhile and it will keep for a few days in the fridge.

6 raw beetroot/beets
500 ml/2 cups apple juice
50 g/3^1/$_4$ tablespoons tomato ketchup
a dash of chilli/hot sauce (such as Tabasco)

Peel and slice the beetroot/beets into thin slices – you may wish to wear disposable gloves to do this to avoid staining your fingers. Put the slices in a pan and cover with about 300 ml/1^1/$_4$ cups of the apple juice.

Bring to a low simmer and cook for 45 minutes until the beetroot/beets offer no resistance when prodded with a sharp knife.

Add the remaining apple juice, tomato ketchup and chilli/hot sauce. Pour into a juicer and process until smooth.

Cover and chill in the fridge for 1 hour, stir then serve.

Pear, beetroot and elderflower

PREPARE: **5 MINUTES** SERVES: **4**

Pear and elderflower is a classic combination. Elderflower has a unique and wonderful flavour and aroma. The season only lasts a couple of months but the flowers can be kept frozen for a few months longer. The addition of lemon juice balances the flavours and stops the pear juice from oxidizing and discolouring. The beetroot/beet adds a depth of flavour and a lovely pink colouring.

6 pears
a bunch of fresh or frozen elderflowers
1 small cooked and peeled red beetroot/beet
freshly squeezed juice of 1 lemon
1–3 teaspoons runny honey

Pears vary in flavour and sweetness quite a lot depending on variety and level of ripeness; choose according to whether you like them hard and less sweet or soft and sugary.

Trim the tops of the pears to remove the stalks and any woody pieces. Roughly chop and place them in the juicer, add the elderflowers, beetroot/beet and lemon juice. Process the mixture until smooth. Add a little honey to taste, approximately 1–3 teaspoons, and process again to combine.

Fennel and orange

PREPARE: **5 MINUTES (PLUS RESTING TIME)** SERVES: **4**

I love the fresh, aniseed flavour of fennel and the combination of fennel and orange is an extraordinary blend of flavours that marry together well.

2 fennel bulbs
grated zest of 2 oranges
freshly squeezed juice of 6 oranges
1 orange, sliced

Trim the base off the fennel bulbs and discard; keep a few fronds for decoration and roughly chop the rest of the bulb into 5-mm/^{1}/$_4$-inch slices. Put in a large mixing bowl with the orange zest and pour the orange juice over. Leave in the fridge for at least 1 hour for the orange juice to tenderize the fennel.

Pour the mixture into a juicer and process. Fennel can be quite tough so you might need to strain the juice through a fine mesh sieve/strainer to remove any larger pieces of fennel.

Serve over ice, decorated with fennel fronds and a slice of orange.

Roots

CARROT • PARSNIP • BEETROOT/BEETS • CELERIAC/CELERY ROOT

Root vegetables are every chef's secret weapon. They provide balance to dishes, with savoury flavours from beetroot/beets, swede/rutabaga and celeriac/celery root, and sweet flavours from carrots, turnips and parsnips. From simply roasting in a variety of ways to make the most of each root vegetable on page 22, to juicing on page 11 and a more technical agar agar-set terrine of carrot and beetroot/beets on page 14, I have tried to bring out the best of their wonderful flavours.

Like most people, I do love something deep-fried and the Tumbleweed Tempura on page 17 uses the sweetness of cooked carrots and onions to balance the earthy flavours of kale and potatoes – you will not be able to stop eating the tumbleweed parcels once you start!

I often serve the Beetroot Soup with Goat's Cheese Cream on page 17 in my restaurant as a surprise course on our tasting menu, the surprise and delight from customers who have never eaten cooked beetroot/beets before is fun to see and to share with them. That and the shock value of a dark purple soup, make this a fun way to start a meal.

Carrot and beetroot terrine

PREPARE: **20 MINUTES**   COOK: **45 MINUTES (PLUS 6 HOURS SETTING TIME)**   SERVES: **8**

This is not only vibrant in colour, it is in flavour, too. Sweet and spicy carrots and earthy, deeply flavoured beetroot/beets make a wonderfully rich terrine. Serve hot, dressed with fennel fronds and topped off with a little freshly grated horseradish.

1 kg/2¼ lbs. fresh uncooked beetroot/beets, peeled

500 ml/2 cups beetroot/beet juice

200 ml/¾ cup ruby Port

1 kg/2¼ lbs. carrots, peeled

250 ml/1 cup apple juice

1 star anise

12 g/4 teaspoons agar agar (setting agent)

table salt, to season

TO SERVE

freshly grated horseradish

fennel fronds (optional)

a terrine or loaf pan lined with clingfilm/plastic wrap

Put the beetroot/beets in a saucepan with the beetroot/beet juice and ruby Port, add a little water if needed to just cover the beetroot/beets. Set the pan over a medium heat and simmer for approximately 40 minutes until the beetroot/beets are softened and cooked through. Remove the beetroot/beets using a slotted spoon and put in a large bowl to cool. Save the cooking liquor and set aside.

Meanwhile, put the carrots in a saucepan with the apple juice and star anise, adding enough water to just cover the carrots. Set the pan over a medium heat and simmer for 15–20 minutes until the carrots are soft but still hold their shape.

Remove the carrots using a slotted spoon and put in a large bowl to cool. Save the cooking liquor, discard the star anise and set aside.

Simmer the beetroot/beet cooking liquor until it has reduced by half its volume, season with a small pinch of salt and remove from the heat.

Finely slice the cooked carrots. Layer the carrot in the terrine or loaf pan to form tightly packed layers about halfway up.

Add 6 g/2 teaspoons of agar agar to 500 ml/2 cups of the carrot cooking liquor, set over a medium heat and bring to a low simmer. Whisk to combine, then pour over the carrot layer till just covered.

Put in the fridge to set – this will take 2–3 hours.

Once the carrot layers have set firm, slice the beetroot/beets and layer over the carrot to fill the terrine or loaf pan.

Bring the beetroot/beet cooking liquor to a low simmer over a medium heat. Add 6 g/2 teaspoons of agar agar and whisk to combine. Pour the liquor slowly, while hot, over the beetroot/beets until just covered. The hot beetroot/beet liquor will melt a little of the carrot jelly to bind the two layers together.

Return to the fridge to set firm – this will take 2–3 hours.

Preheat the oven to 70°C (160°F) Gas ¼ if serving warm. Cook in the preheated oven for 5 minutes or so.

Whether hot or cold, slice with a very sharp knife and serve with a tiny amount of fresh horseradish finely grated over the top.

Beetroot soup with goat's cheese cream

PREPARE: **5 MINUTES** COOK: **10 MINUTES** SERVES: **4**

Beetroot/beets and apple is one of those unexpected flavour combinations that works perfectly. This simple soup never fails to delight diners in my restaurant. The goat's cheese cream adds a sharpness and saltiness to the soup.

600 g/1¼ lbs. pre-cooked red beetroot/beets

400 ml/1⅔ cups apple juice

20 ml/1½ tablespoons double/heavy cream

100 g/3½ oz. soft goat's cheese

Roughly chop the beetroot/beets into 1-cm/⅜-inch cubes and put into a saucepan with the apple juice. Set over a medium heat and bring to a low simmer for 5 minutes then purée using a handheld electric blender to produce a smooth soup.

Whisk the cream and goat's cheese together in a separate bowl to form a thick cream.

To serve, pour the soup into bowls and, using two spoons, form the goat's cheese cream into a quenelle. Place on top of the soup and serve immediately.

Tumbleweed tempura

PREPARE: **15 MINUTES** COOK: **5 MINUTES** SERVES: **4**

A fun way to eat vegetables that's mouthwateringly delicious. The tempura batter is light and crispy and works really well with vegetables.

2 potatoes, spiralized or very thinly sliced into strips

2 carrots, spiralized or very thinly sliced into strips

1 onion, thinly sliced into strips

2 kale leaves, thinly sliced into strips

1 litre/quart vegetable oil

100 g/1 cup cornflour/cornstarch

100 g/¾ cup plain/all-purpose flour

1 teaspoon table salt

100 ml/⅓ cup sparkling water

freshly ground black pepper, to season

aioli and tomato ketchup, to serve

Mix the potato, carrot, onion and kale strips together and season with a generous pinch of pepper.

Pour the vegetable oil into a deep-fryer or chip pan and bring to a temperature of 180°C (350°F).

Put the cornflour/cornstarch, plain/all-purpose flour and table salt into a large mixing bowl and loosely mix together. Add the sparkling water and use the fingertips of one hand to mix them until they form a batter.

With the 'clean' hand, bunch small handfuls of the vegetables into balls and place in the batter. Coat the ball with the batter, shake off any excess and carefully place in the preheated deep-fryer or chip pan.

Cook for 5 minutes, or until it is just starting to turn golden. Remove and drain on paper towels for a minute, then serve with a little aioli and tomato ketchup to dip them into.

Celeriac remoulade with heritage beetroot and fennel

PREPARE: **60 MINUTES** COOK: **45 MINUTES** SERVES: **4**

The balance of the flavours is the key to this dish. The wonderful earthy, sweet flavours of the beetroot/beets, the peppery celeriac/celery root, the nutty oil and the fragrant fennel fronds to finish combine for melt-in-the-mouth perfection.

8 beetroot/beets of various colours

1 celeriac/celery root

1 teaspoon English mustard

2–3 dashes of Tabasco sauce

1 bag of fresh rocket/arugula

fennel fronds, to serve

salt, to season

MAYONNAISE (OR SUBSTITUTE NO-EGG MAYONNAISE, PAGE 158)

200 ml/³/4 cup first-press rapeseed oil, plus extra to serve

1 egg

1 teaspoon white wine vinegar

a pinch of table salt

First, make the mayonnaise for the remoulade; you will need a handheld electric blender and a jug/pitcher of about 300-ml/10-oz. capacity that is only slightly larger in diameter than the blade end of the blender to follow this method.

Add the oil, egg, vinegar and salt to the jug/pitcher and wait for the egg to settle to the bottom, capture the egg under the base of the blender and, in short bursts of 2–3 seconds, pulse to emulsify the oil and egg together to form mayonnaise. Continue pulsing and slowly draw it up the jug/pitcher until all of the oil is combined to make a thick, yellow mayonnaise.

Alternatively use 250 ml/1 cup of store-bought mayonnaise or the No-egg Mayonnaise on page 158.

Preheat the oven to 180°C (350°F) Gas 4.

To prepare the beetroot/beets, heavily salt them and wrap tightly in foil. Place on the middle shelf of the preheated oven and roast for about 45 minutes. Test if they're cooked through by poking with a toothpick; it should be soft to skewer. Remove from the oven, unwrap from the foil and leave to cool for 30 minutes. Carefully peel off the outer layer, which should fall away easily, leaving you with beautifully cooked beetroot/beets. Slice into thin slices and set aside.

To make the remoulade, peel the celeriac/celery root and carefully chop into matchstick-sized pieces. Mix with the mayonnaise. Add a generous teaspoon of English mustard and a few dashes of Tabasco, to taste.

Assemble a handful of rocket/arugula on each plate. Spoon the remoulade over and arrange the sliced beetroot on top. Drizzle with a little rapeseed oil and decorate with fennel fronds.

Smoked parsnip, pear and Stilton salad

PREPARE: **15 MINUTES** COOK: **30 MINUTES** SERVES: **4**

This marriage of traditional English flavours makes a delightful light warm salad. Have fun making a simple home smoker and experiment with smoking other ingredients; root vegetables take smoke very well.

300 g/³/₄ lb. parsnips, peeled and sliced lengthways

2 just-ripe pears, peeled and cut lengthways into quarters, seeds removed

1 chicory/Belgian endive, trimmed into leaves

100 g/1 cup walnut halves

1 teaspoon runny honey or agave syrup

100 g/3¹/₂ oz. Stilton or hard blue cheese

sea salt, to season

vegetable oil, for coating and frying

SMOKE

1 tablespoon white sugar

2 tablespoons white rice

2 tablespoons loose Earl Grey tea leaves

Preheat the oven to 180°C (350°F) Gas 4.

Lightly tea-smoke the parsnips following the method below for 5 minutes. Once smoked, rub them with vegetable oil. Put in a roasting pan and roast in the preheated oven for 20 minutes.

Add a little vegetable oil to a frying pan/skillet and set over a medium heat. Add the pears, chicory/Belgian endive leaves and walnuts. Cook for about 5 minutes, turning regularly to cook evenly. Remove from the heat, drizzle with the honey and turn the ingredients gently in the pan, coating them in the pan juices and adding just a hint of honey flavour. Sprinkle with a good pinch of sea salt to season.

Serve the smoked parsnips and the pan-fried pears, walnuts and chicory/Belgian endive on warm plates. Crumble the Stilton into bite-sized pieces and scatter around the salad.

Home smoking: To make a smoker, put the sugar and rice and the Earl Grey tea in the base of a wok. Cover the mixture with two layers of foil, with a piece of crumpled foil between the layers making a gap of about 1 cm/³/₈ inch. This will allow the smoke to seep around the edges of the foil.

Set the wok over a high heat. Rest the parsnips (or other vegetables) on top of the foil and cover the wok with a lid. Leave to smoke for five minutes. Once smoked, finish cooking the parsnips according to the recipe above.

Tip: If you smoke food after cooking it, rather than before, the flavour will be too harsh; the smokiness needs to be mellowed by cooking in butter or oil after smoking.

The perfect roast veg

PREPARE: **30 MINUTES** COOK: **30 MINUTES** SERVES: **4**

As a great alternative to a meat roast, this dish may take a little bit of preparation but the end result is a beautiful plate of food with each vegetable cooked to its full, delicious potential.

4 carrots, unpeeled

1 star anise

4 large roasting potatoes, peeled and cut in half

a knob/pat of unsalted butter

4 parsnips, peeled and cut into quarters lengthways

1 celeriac/celery root, peeled and diced into 1-cm/$^3/_8$-inch cubes

1 small pumpkin, unpeeled and sliced into 2-cm/$^3/_4$-inch wedges

1 large sweet potato, peeled and sliced into 2-cm/$^3/_4$-inch rounds

2 onions, trimmed and quartered

a drizzle of runny honey

a pinch of cumin seeds

1 teaspoon miso paste

fresh marjoram, thyme and sage leaves, to season

table salt, to season

ground white pepper, to season

vegetable oil, to coat

Preheat the oven to 180°C (350°F) Gas 4.

Scrub the carrots with a wire scourer to clean off all the dirt and make them rough. Put in a saucepan of cold salted water and add the star anise. Set over a medium heat and bring to a low simmer for 10 minutes, then remove from the water using a slotted spoon and leave to cool. Slice in half lengthways, rub with a little vegetable oil and place in a large oven dish with a light covering of salt to season, leaving room for all the other vegetables.

Put the potatoes in a saucepan of cold salted water. Set over a medium heat and bring to a low simmer for about 15 minutes until they are just starting to flake and break up. Drain the potatoes using a fine mesh sieve/strainer and set over the warm pan (no longer on the heat) for 10 minutes to dry out completely. Toss with a knob/pat of butter and add a pinch of salt and white pepper while they are still warm. Transfer to the oven dish with the carrots.

Rub a little vegetable oil over the parsnips and then a little honey to form a thin glaze. Put in the oven dish and sprinkle with a little salt to season.

Toss the celeriac/celery root cubes with some vegetable oil and $^1/_2$ teaspoon of salt and transfer to the oven dish.

Remove any seeds from the pumpkin slices, rub with vegetable oil to coat, then sprinkle lightly with cumin seeds. Transfer to the oven dish and arrange skin-side down.

Rub the sweet potato slices with vegetable oil, then rub the flesh with the miso paste. Transfer to the oven dish.

Add the onion and drizzle with a little vegetable oil.

Sprinkle a few marjoram, sage and thyme leaves over the top and cook in the preheated oven for 30–40 minutes or until the potatoes are golden brown.

Remove from the oven and serve.

Spring pistou soup

PREPARE: **20 MINUTES** COOK: **1 HOUR** SERVES: **4**

The essence of this dish is a deeply flavoured but clean, clear consommé or stock, that should surprise and delight the palate. Try serving the consommé in a separate jug/pitcher or glass teapot, then pouring over a garlicky pesto and perfectly cooked vegetables.

2 carrots, peeled and chopped into matchsticks

1 celeriac/celery root, peeled and chopped into 6-mm/¼-inch cubes

a pinch of sea salt

60 g/½ cup frozen peas (defrosted)

a bunch of flowering chives and finely chopped fresh chives, to decorate

PESTO

200 g/1½ cups unsalted cashew nuts

2 garlic cloves

grated zest of 1 lemon and freshly squeezed juice of ½

leaves of a medium bunch of fresh basil

a pinch of sea salt

olive oil, to drizzle

CONSOMMÉ

2 carrots, peeled and chopped into 5-mm/¼-inch cubes

4 celery sticks, chopped into 5-mm/¼-inch cubes

1 onion, chopped into 5-mm/¼-inch cubes

25 ml/1½ tablespoons sherry

a pinch of sea salt

Preheat the oven to 140°C (275°F) Gas 1.

To make the pesto, put the cashew nuts and garlic on a baking sheet and roast in a preheated oven for 20 minutes. Transfer to a food processor and add the lemon zest, juice, basil and the salt. Pulse the mixture, then drizzle in a little olive oil as necessary to form a coarse pesto that will hold when pressed together between two spoons. This can be stored in an airtight container in the fridge for up to 5 days.

To make the consommé, put the carrot, celery and onion cubes into a saucepan with 800 ml/3⅓ cups of water and the sherry. Set over a medium heat until it reaches a low simmer, then reduce the heat to just below simmering and leave at this temperature for about 1 hour. Strain the liquid consommé through a fine mesh sieve/strainer into a jug/pitcher, add the salt and gently stir. Set aside until ready to serve.

Put the carrot matchsticks and celeriac/celery root cubes into a saucepan, cover with water, add the salt and set over a medium–high heat. Bring to a rolling boil for 2 minutes, strain and run under cold water to stop them cooking. Set aside until ready to serve.

Use two spoons to form quenelles of pesto and place in the centre of the serving bowls. Assemble the cooked, cubed vegetables and the defrosted peas around them. Reheat the consommé in a saucepan set over a high heat until piping hot and, at the table, pour it over the pesto and vegetables. Decorate with finely chopped chives and chive flowers.

Brassicas and greens

**CAULIFLOWER • CABBAGE • PAK CHOI/BOK CHOY
KALE • BROCCOLI • CHARD**

We are finally starting to rediscover brassicas and greens. Open any health food or juice book and there are recipes full of kale and cauliflower. We all too often forget to mention that they are delicious when treated with respect, not just healthy.

Cauliflower is just stunning when raw or cooked. I've puréed it in a delicious Cauliflower and Truffle Pâté on page 29, roasted it with Moroccan flavours of pomegranate, preserved lemon and pine nuts on page 30 and griddled then poached it in a cheese sauce for an alternative to a standard Cauliflower Cheese on page 33.

When preparing cauliflower, save the off-cuts and blitz them for a second or two in a food processor to make cauliflower rice. Simply steamed for a couple of minutes and you have a tasty rice replacement for a curry, or try it grilled/broiled on toast with some cheese sprinkled on top for a truly decadent lunch of cauliflower cheese on toast. Use the stems and make matchsticks for dipping in hummous, or a sour cream dip. Above all, don't waste any of this delicious vegetable.

Looking back at the recipes, I realize I have favoured cauliflower over broccoli a little. This reflects the season of when this book was written more than anything else, so over the winter months substitute broccoli for any of the cauliflower recipes because it's just as delicious.

Cauliflower and truffle pâté with pea shoots

PREPARE: **10 MINUTES** COOK: **20 MINUTES** SERVES: **4**

Cauliflower is a hugely versatile vegetable. Roasting gives it a nuttiness that balances well with the richness of truffle to make a gorgeous pâté.

½ cauliflower

50 ml/3 tablespoons double/heavy cream

1 teaspoon truffle oil

vegetable oil, to drizzle

table salt, to season

8 slices sourdough or seeded bread, to serve

a handful of pea shoots, to serve (optional)

Preheat the oven to 180°C (350°F) Gas 4.

To prepare the cauliflower, chop into pieces about 1 cm/⅜ inch. Put in a saucepan, cover with water and set over a low–medium heat. Simmer for 5 minutes, before draining.

Scatter the cauliflower onto a baking sheet, drizzle with a little vegetable oil and sprinkle with salt. Roast in the preheated oven for 10–12 minutes until just starting to turn golden.

Remove from the oven and return the cauliflower to the saucepan, add the cream and a generous pinch of salt. Purée using a handheld electric blender until it resembles cottage cheese in consistency. Set aside to cool, then put in the fridge and, once it has cooled completely, add a dash of truffle oil and stir to incorporate; the pâté is finished. It can now be stored in a sealed container, in the fridge, for up to four days.

Toast the sourdough or seeded bread slices.

To serve, spread the pâté on toasts and top with pea shoots.

Moroccan roasted cauliflower

PREPARE: **5 MINUTES** COOK: **40 MINUTES** SERVES **4**

Cauliflower takes strong flavours like spices well as it creates a savoury depth to the dish. I've used spices to add heat and flavour with the orange, pomegranate and pine nuts to make bursts of flavour. The jewel-toned rose petals and pomegranate combine with the other ingredients to bring flashes of colour and North African aromas, and make this dish an exciting centrepiece for a family dinner.

1 cauliflower

200 g/1¾ sticks butter

50 g/¼ cup tahini

½ teaspoon ground cinnamon

½ teaspoon ground cumin

1 teaspoon ground turmeric

1 teaspoon fennel seeds

1 teaspoon runny honey

½ preserved lemon, finely chopped

100 g/¾ cup pine nuts

grated zest and freshly squeezed juice of 1 orange

seeds from 1 pomegranate

petals from two tea roses

a small bunch of fresh flat-leaf parsley

freshly ground black pepper, to season

Preheat the oven to 160°C (325°F) Gas 3.

Remove the outer leaves and put the whole cauliflower into a large saucepan of cold, salted water. Set over a medium heat and bring to a simmer. Continue simmering for 5 minutes. Remove from the heat, drain off the water and leave the cauliflower to steam dry in a colander set over the hot pan for 10 minutes.

In a small saucepan, gently melt the butter, then add the tahini, ground cinnamon, cumin, turmeric, fennel seeds and honey. Stir to combine.

Transfer the cauliflower to a casserole dish and spoon the seasoned butter over the top. Add the finely chopped preserved lemon.

Put in the preheated oven and roast for 10 minutes. Baste the cauliflower with the juices from the casserole dish, then roast for another 10 minutes. Baste again and add the pine nuts. Turn the oven up to 220°C (425°F) Gas 7 and roast for a further 5 minutes; this will start to char the cauliflower and roast the pine nuts.

Remove the casserole dish from the oven. Spoon the cauliflower onto a large serving bowl or platter and cut into portions. Spoon over the casserole juices, lemon pieces and pine nuts, followed by the orange juice and zest, pomegranate seeds, a good pinch of black pepper, rose petals and a few torn parsley leaves.

Serve as a centrepiece on the table or plate onto individual serving plates.

Cauliflower cheese

PREPARE: **30 MINUTES** COOK: **20 MINUTES** SERVES: **4**

This recipe is all about the cheese. Don't panic if you don't have all four cheeses, just increase the amount of cheeses you do have to the same overall weight. However, if you do have all four, the combination of their flavours and textures makes an amazing sticky lava flow of cheese that cannot be beaten.

2 large cauliflower

30 g/2 tablespoons butter

30 g/2 tablespoons plain/all-purpose flour

500 ml/2 cups whole milk

100 g/1¼ cups grated strong Cheddar cheese

100 g/1 cup grated Gruyère cheese

50 g/⅔ cup grated Parmesan cheese

120 g/1 cup sliced mozzarella cheese

1–2 teaspoons English mustard

1–2 splashes of Tabasco sauce, to season

a pinch of smoked paprika

table salt, to season

olive oil, to coat

tomato salad, to serve

Preheat the oven to 160°C (325°F) Gas 3.

Prepare the cauliflower by trimming the leaves off, then slicing across the base in 2-cm/¾-inch slices, like slicing a loaf of bread. Lightly oil the cauliflower slices on both sides and season with a little salt.

Preheat a griddle pan over a medium heat, then cook the cauliflower slices for 2–3 minutes on each side, to just char and par-cook them. This should leave the cauliflower cooked one-third of the way through on each side.

Lay the slices in a casserole dish, overlapping to fit them all in.

To make the sauce, begin by making a roux. Put the butter and flour in a dry saucepan and set over a medium heat until the mixture forms crumbs and is just starting to colour. Slowly, add about 125 ml/½ cup of milk and whisk to combine into a smooth, thick paste. With the pan still on the heat, keep adding the milk 125 ml/½ cup at a time and whisk together to combine until all of the milk has been added to the sauce and it is thin and smooth.

Reduce to a low heat and add two-thirds of the Cheddar, Gruyère and Parmesan cheeses to the sauce. Whisk gently until the sauce is smooth, then add the mozzarella cheese. Whisk until the cheese has melted and you have a smooth sauce.

Add a large teaspoon of mustard, a generous splash of Tabasco sauce and a pinch of salt, and whisk together. Taste the sauce and add more mustard, Tabasco sauce or salt as you like it.

Pour the sauce over the cauliflower, then sprinkle the remaining cheese over and finish with the smoked paprika to decorate and add a hint of smoke. At this stage, you can store the cauliflower cheese in a fridge for up to 2 days.

Bake in the preheated oven for 15 minutes (20 minutes if it has been chilled in the fridge). Check that it is cooked by probing with a fork to ensure there is no hard centre. Turn the oven up to 200°C (400°F) Gas 6 for 5 minutes to brown the cheese topping.

Serve 2–3 slices of cauliflower with the sauce per person with a tomato salad on the side.

Savoy cabbage ratatouille parcels

PREPARE: **30 MINUTES** COOK: **20 MINUTES** SERVES: **4**

This is my take on the classic Ratatouille Niçoise. It has been designed to look extraordinary but by taking care to cook each element separately and then combine them in the parcels, the flavours of each ingredient are enhanced.

4 large leaves of savoy cabbage

1 aubergine/eggplant, sliced into 1-cm/³⁄₈-inch rounds

2 red onions, finely diced

1 onion, finely diced

1 red (bell) pepper, deseeded and finely diced

1 yellow (bell) pepper, deseeded and finely diced

1 courgette/zucchini, finely diced

olive oil, for frying

table salt, to season

a small bunch of fresh marjoram, to serve

TOMATO SAUCE

2 garlic cloves

1 teaspoon capers

400 g/2 cups canned chopped tomatoes

1 teaspoon white sugar

olive oil, for frying

table salt, to season

Preheat the oven to 160°C (325°F) Gas 3.

To make the tomato sauce, pour enough olive oil to coat the bottom of a small saucepan and add the garlic and capers. Set over a low heat to cook the garlic and capers until they are just starting to turn golden brown. Add the canned tomatoes and sugar, and leave to simmer on low for 10 minutes.

Using a handheld electric blender, purée the mixture to a smooth consistency and season with a pinch or two of table salt. Pour the mixture through a fine mesh sieve/strainer into a saucepan and set aside.

Put the savoy cabbage leaves in a pan of boiling salted water and blanch for 2 minutes, then remove and pat dry with paper towels.

Preheat a frying pan/skillet over a high heat. Drizzle a little oil over the aubergine/eggplant slices, then carefully place them into the very hot pan/skillet and cook until they're just starting to blacken. Repeat on the other side, then remove from the heat and allow to cool. Chop and dice the slices into about 5-mm/¹⁄₄-inch pieces.

Add a light covering of oil to a frying pan/skillet. Set over a low heat and add the onions and (bell) peppers. Cover with a generous pinch of salt and leave to cook gently until the onions are translucent – this may take about 3–5 minutes. Add the courgette/zucchini and cook for another couple of minutes stirring gently. Remove from the heat, add the aubergine/eggplant pieces and gently stir to make the ratatouille.

Place the savoy cabbage leaves into large ramekins, allowing the edges of the leaves to hang over the sides. Fill with the ratatouille mixture and fold the edges over to seal. Cover the top with foil to hold everything together.

Bake the parcels in the preheated oven for 20 minutes. Gently heat the saucepan of tomato sauce at the same time. Once cooked, carefully remove the foil and turn the parcels out onto large soup plates. Spoon the tomato sauce around the edge.

Decorate with fresh marjoram flowers and leaves and serve.

Pak choi with chilli, orange and pomegranate

PREPARE: **5 MINUTES** COOK: **6 MINUTES** SERVES: **4**

Pak choi/bok choy, pan-fried in a little sesame oil, is one of my favourite things to eat on its own. Here I've added some heat with a chilli/chile and some sweetness to make a delicious dish for a light lunch or an appetizer for a dinner party.

4 pak choi/bok choy

2 oranges

1 red chilli/chile

seeds of 1 pomegranate

sesame oil, to coat

sea salt, to season

Remove the outer leaves and slice the pak choi/bok choy in half. Rub the halves with sesame oil.

Zest the oranges and set aside. Cut the peel and pith from the oranges, then cut the segments out using a small, sharp knife between the membranes.

Finely slice the chilli/chile on the diagonal.

Preheat a large, heavy-based saucepan over a high heat until it is scalding hot. Carefully place the pak choi/bok choy in flat-side down and leave for 2–3 minutes until it is starting to char.

Turn the pak choi/bok choy over and, after 1 minute, take off the heat. Add the orange segments, sliced chilli/chile and pomegranate seeds. Stir quickly for 2 minutes to stop any of the ingredients burning and serve immediately on warm plates. Sprinkle with a little reserved orange zest and sea salt to taste.

Kale gnocchi with kale crisps

PREPARE: **45 MINUTES** COOK: **20 MINUTES** SERVES: **4**

Kale has wonderful strong flavours and this recipe is intended to show it off at its absolute best.

a large bunch of kale

1 teaspoon balsamic vinegar

1 garlic clove, crushed

750 g/1³/4 lbs. baking potatoes, peeled and roughly chopped into small pieces

2 egg yolks

2–3 tablespoons plain/all-purpose flour

50 g/¹/3 cup frozen peas

100 g/¹/2 cup Kale Pesto (page 168)

sesame oil, to coat, plus extra for frying

vegetable oil, for frying

sea salt, to season

Preheat the oven to 160°C (325°F) Gas 3.

To make the crisps, roughly chop half of the kale into pieces the size of potato crisps/chips, removing the central stem. Toss with several teaspoons of sesame oil, the balsamic vinegar and garlic to just coat. Spread the kale out on a baking sheet and bake in the preheated oven for 7 minutes or until just starting to colour. Remove from the oven and leave at room temperature to finish crisping up. Sprinkle with sea salt to taste and store in an airtight container if you are not using them straight away.

To make the gnocchi, roughly chop the remaining kale and put in a saucepan with the diced potatoes. Just cover with cold water, season with a generous pinch of salt and set over a medium heat. Bring to a low simmer for about 8–10 minutes, until the potatoes are just starting to break up.

Drain the potatoes and kale using a sieve/strainer and leave suspended over the saucepan to drain fully and dry slightly for 10 minutes.

Transfer the cooked potatoes and kale to a food processor, add the egg yolks and pulse to a smooth paste but take care not to over-blend. Add 2 tablespoons of flour and pulse a few times to bring the mixture together. Tip the dough out and form a rough ball. Add more flour, sparingly, if needed, until the mixture comes together easily as a ball.

Form the dough into a sausage shape and roll up in baking parchment or clingfilm/plastic wrap. Chill in the fridge for at least 30 minutes, to firm up.

Roll the dough into a long sausage shape, the thickness of your thumb on a lightly floured surface. Slice at 2.5-cm/1-inch intervals and press lightly with a fork to just flatten.

Bring a pan of salted water to a gentle simmer over a medium heat and add the gnocchi. Leave until they start to float, remove and set aside to cool. Separate the gnocchi while cooling or they will stick together. The gnocchi can be kept for several days at this stage; lightly drizzle with oil to prevent drying and keep chilled.

When ready to serve, pan fry the gnocchi in a mixture of vegetable oil and a little sesame oil until browned. Add the peas to the pan, season with a pinch of sea salt and stir through the kale pesto. Spoon onto the plates, finish with a generous covering of kale crisps and serve.

Sprouting broccoli, hazelnuts and fondant potatoes

PREPARE: **15 MINUTES** COOK: **60 MINUTES** SERVES: **4**

I do love a fondant potato... it's the mix of the best roast and baked potato flavours imaginable. Here, I've paired it with sprouting broccoli and freshly roasted hazelnuts for a delicious spring or autumnal/fall dish.

4 large potatoes, peeled

1 litre/quart vegetable stock

200 g/1¾ sticks butter

100 g/¾ cup peeled hazelnuts

200 g/½ lb. sprouting broccoli

2–3 teaspoons balsamic vinegar

vegetable oil, to coat

sea salt and ground black pepper, to season

Preheat the oven to 180°C (350°F) Gas 4.

Trim each potato into roughly the shape of a bar of soap. Put in a large ovenproof saucepan with the vegetable stock and butter. Bring to a low simmer over a medium heat, then cover with a lid.

Simmer for 15 minutes, then transfer the saucepan, uncovered, to the preheated oven and cook for 20 minutes. Carefully turn the potatoes over, they should be golden on the top and most of the stock should have cooked off. Turn the oven down to 140°C (275°F) Gas 1 and cook for a further 30 minutes until the potatoes are golden and all of the stock has evaporated.

Scatter the hazelnuts on a baking sheet and cook in the oven for the last 20 minutes.

Meanwhile, lightly oil the sprouting broccoli. Preheat an ovenproof griddle pan over a high heat and cook the sprouting broccoli to just blacken it. Drizzle with balsamic vinegar and sprinkle with sea salt, cover and place the pan in the oven for the last 10 minutes.

Take everything from the oven. Transfer the hazelnuts to a freezer bag, seal and tap them with the end of a rolling pin to just break them up a little.

To serve, arrange the fondant potatoes on warm plates, then add the sprouting broccoli, followed by a generous 1–2 tablespoons of the broken hazelnuts. Finish by sprinkling a good pinch of sea salt and black pepper over the plate and a drizzle of the pan juices.

Cheese and pickles

PREPARE: **30 MINUTES** COOK: **20 MINUTES** SERVES: **4**

This dish looks complicated but it's all in the preparation. A version of a dish we serve at the restaurant, it makes a great dinner party appetizer. The beetroot/beet is not pickled because, well, it's not my favourite thing. Nevertheless, it's a fantastic vegetable and the earthy flavour and colour contrast well with the pickles and the goat's cheese.

2 eggs

250 g/9 oz. pre-cooked whole beetroot/beets

100 g/3½ oz. soft goat's cheese

Vegetable Pickles (page 166)

150 g/5½ oz. hard goat's cheese, sliced into four pieces

caster/granulated sugar, to sprinkle

a pinch of table salt

nasturtium leaves and flowers, to serve

a chef's blow torch (optional)

Place the eggs in a pan of boiling water and cook them for 4 minutes for soft-boiled/soft-cooked, or 7 minutes for hard-boiled/hard-cooked. Lift them out using a slotted spoon, replace the boiling water with cold, gently tap the eggs to crack the shell all over, then place them back in the cold water for a few minutes to cool and to let the shells loosen. Peel and set aside.

Finely dice one of the beetroots/beets into 5-mm/¼-inch cubes; save the off-cuts. To make a beetroot/beet purée, take the remaining beetroot/beets and off-cuts, roughly chop them and put into a pan. Add water, just enough to cover them, and set over a medium heat. Bring to the boil and simmer for 10 minutes. Take off the heat, drain and carefully, using a handheld electric blender, whizz until they form a smooth paste. Add a pinch of salt to season and set aside.

To assemble, drop a tablespoon of the beetroot/beet purée at one end of each plate and, using the side of the spoon, make a cheffy swoop across them. Crumble the soft goat's cheese around each plate. Slice the peeled eggs in half and place one half on each plate. Decorate with the mixed pickled vegetables and beetroot/beet cubes. (The golden rule for presentation is always use odd numbers, 3 or 5 of each in an interesting pattern around the plate will look wonderful.)

Sprinkle the hard goat's cheese with a thin layer of caster/granulated sugar, then caramelize with a chef's blow torch or under a hot grill/broiler for 30 seconds. Transfer to the dressed plates and scatter around a few nasturtium leaves and flowers.

Rainbow chard and Comté quiche

PREPARE: **15 MINUTES** COOK: **80 MINUTES** SERVES: **4**

Chard and Comté quiche is a classic French dish; my recipe uses rainbow chard for added colour. If you can't find Comté, or struggle to find a vegetarian Comté-style cheese, it can be substituted with Gruyère cheese.

200 g/7 oz. all-butter shortcrust pastry

2 shallots, finely diced

a large bunch of rainbow chard, roughly chopped

150 g/5 oz. Comté cheese

6 eggs

200 ml/$^3/_4$ cup double/heavy cream

200 ml/$^3/_4$ cup whole milk

a pinch of ground mace

butter, for frying

a pinch of table salt

a pinch of ground black pepper

green salad, to serve (optional)

a deep fluted 25-cm/10-inch diameter tart pan, greased

Preheat the oven to 180°C (350°F) Gas 4.

Roll the pastry out on a lightly floured surface to a thickness of about 3 mm/$^1/_8$ inch. Gently drape it over a rolling pin and transfer to the tart pan, covering it and overlapping the sides. With the pastry in place, use a fork to prick the base repeatedly, about 5 mm/$^1/_4$ inch apart, then set in the refrigerator for 15 minutes to firm up.

Blind bake in the preheated oven for 10 minutes to set the pastry and make the quiche base. Remove and trim off any excess pastry around the top to create a smooth edge. Leave the oven on but turn it down to 160°C (325°F) Gas 3.

Put the shallots in a large frying pan/skillet with enough butter to cover the base when heated. Set over a high heat until the butter is sizzling, then add the chard, cooking and turning it for a few minutes, until it begins to wilt.

Transfer the chard and shallot mixture in a sieve/strainer and, using the back of a wooden spoon, squeeze out any excess liquid.

Cover the base of the quiche with the chard and shallot mixture, then finely grate the Comté cheese over the top.

Whisk together the eggs, cream, milk, mace, salt and pepper. Pour into the quiche base, until just below the rim.

Bake in the oven for 45–50 minutes, until the mixture just starts to set in the middle. Remove from the oven and rest for 10 minutes to finish cooking.

Serve hot or cold with a green salad if desired.

Thai-style vegetables en papillote with noodles

PREPARE: **20 MINUTES** COOK: **20 MINUTES** SERVES: **4**

A lovely fusion dish using the classic Pad Thai as inspiration. I love the perfumed aromas from the rice wine, aromatic lemon grass and galangal root. You can usually find daikon and galangal in a good Asian food store; but if you can't, this dish still works well with radishes and ginger instead.

4 carrots, finely chopped into matchsticks

2 shallots, finely sliced

2 pak choi/bok choy, leaves separated and centres halved

1 daikon radish, peeled and finely sliced or 14–16 red radishes, finely sliced

2 large red chillies/chiles, finely sliced on the diagonal

50 g/½ cup roughly chopped galangal or ginger in 2-cm/¾-inch pieces

2 lemon grass stalks, bruised and sliced into 2-cm/¾-inch pieces

150 g/1⅓ cup trimmed and chopped green beans in 2.5-cm/1-inch pieces

100 ml/⅓ cup rice wine

8 okra, trimmed and sliced into 5-mm/¼-inch pieces

100 g/3½ oz. shiitake mushrooms, stems removed and quartered

a good splash of sesame oil

600 g/21 oz. pre-cooked medium noodles

vegetable oil, for frying

TO SERVE

dark soy sauce

a small bunch of fresh coriander/cilantro

cashew nuts, crushed

Preheat the oven to 180°C (350°F) Gas 4.

To make a papillote bag, cut a rectangle of baking parchment approximately 30 x 45 cm/12 x 18 inches and a piece of foil 40 x 55 cm/16 x 22 inches. Place the baking parchment on top of the foil and fold in half. Seal the sides by folding the foil over several times, capturing the baking parchment inside, forming an envelope.

Carefully place the carrots, shallots, pak choi/bok choy, daikon radish or red radishes, chillies/chiles, galangal or ginger, lemon grass and green beans inside the envelope and add the rice wine. Seal the top and put on a baking sheet. Bake in the preheated oven for 20 minutes.

While the vegetables are cooking prepare the noodles. Preheat a large frying pan/skillet over a high heat with just enough vegetable oil to coat the bottom. When the oil is just starting to shimmer from the heat, add the okra and mushrooms. Cook for 3 minutes, turning occasionally, until the okra is starting to turn golden. Add a good splash of sesame oil and then the noodles. Reduce the heat to low and turn the noodles in the pan to warm them through and mix with the okra and mushrooms.

To serve, place the papillote bag in a large bowl and rest for 5 minutes (don't serve the lemon grass or galangal or ginger pieces). Put the noodles in another large bowl and dress with a little soy sauce. Put the coriander/cilantro leaves and cashew nuts in smaller serving bowls. When you open the papillote bag at the table, it will fill the room with wonderful aromas. Allow your guests to help themselves for the perfect balance.

Tomatoes, peppers and aubergines

TOMATOES • CHILLIES/CHILES • PEPPERS • AUBERGINE/EGGPLANT

There are half a dozen or so ingredients that I could write a whole book about and tomatoes are one of those. They are so versatile, complement so many other ingredients and have been grown and used by many different cultures around the world for centuries, so they fit naturally with many different cuisines. Most of the recipes in this section feature tomatoes, from a fun Bloody Mary Soup on page 50, to a Tabbouleh on page 53 and several pasta dishes (Arrabbiata Quills on page 50, Goat's Cheese and Marjoram Ravioli Marinara and Spaghetti Puttanesca, both on page 54).

The Jambalaya on page 62 makes the most of sweet (bell) peppers and takes me to one of my favourite cuisines, a delicious Creole and Cajun combination that can only come from Southern Louisiana.

Aubergine/eggplant is my 'go-to' ingredient as a result of writing this book; the ragù used in the Aubergine Lasagne on page 61 can be used as a substitute in pretty much any recipe that calls for ground beef, usually with better results. Aubergine/eggplant can take strong flavours but be careful not to overcook it.

Bloody Mary soup

PREPARE: **10 MINUTES** COOK: **40 MINUTES** SERVES: **4**

Perfect on a cold day, or as an appetizer for a dinner party served with a shot of vodka on the side to really warm things up!

2 tablespoons olive oil

2 onions, sliced

2 celery sticks, roughly chopped

1 garlic clove, thinly sliced

800 g/4 cups canned peeled plum tomatoes

2 teaspoons Worcestershire sauce or vegetarian Worcestershire sauce, such as Biona

a generous glug of Tabasco sauce

200 ml/³/4 cup vegetable stock

freshly squeezed juice of ¹/2 lemon

sea salt and freshly ground black pepper, to season

4 celery sticks, to serve

150–200 ml/²/3–³/4 cup vodka (optional)

Pour the oil into a deep saucepan and set over a low heat. Gently fry the onion and celery for 15 minutes, until softened. Add a pinch of salt. Add the garlic and cook for a further 1 minute.

Stir in the tomatoes, Worcestershire sauce or vegetarian Worcestershire sauce, Tabasco and stock. Increase the heat and bring to the boil. Cover and simmer for 20 minutes.

Remove the pan from the heat, allow to cool slightly, then whizz in a blender.

Push the soup through a fine mesh sieve/strainer into a clean saucepan. Taste it and adjust the seasoning with salt, pepper and lemon juice.

Serve with a celery stick and a shot of vodka if you dare.

Arrabbiata quills

PREPARE: **5 MINUTES** COOK: **12 MINUTES** SERVES: **4**

The hot and fresh flavours in this recipe will amaze you... not for the faint-hearted as the dried chilli/hot red pepper flakes pack a punch but perfect with a glass of robust red wine.

300 g/4¹/2 cups bronze-dyed dried penne pasta

extra virgin olive oil, for cooking

4 garlic cloves, crushed

1 brown onion, finely diced

2 teaspoons dried chilli/hot red pepper flakes

150 g/10 tablespoons concentrated tomato purée/paste

500 ml/2 cups vegetable stock

100 g/1¹/2 cups grated Parmesan cheese

a small bunch of fresh basil, to serve

table salt, to season

Half-fill a large saucepan with water and bring to a rolling boil. Add a couple of teaspoons of table salt then the dried pasta. Leave on a rolling boil for one minute less than the cooking time on the packet.

While the pasta is cooking, just cover the base of a large pan with oil and set over a medium heat. Add the garlic and onion with a pinch of salt and cook for a couple of minutes until they start to colour. Add the tomato purée/paste and dried chilli/hot red pepper flakes, and cook for 2–3 minutes before slowly adding the stock, stirring to combine. Continue adding stock until the sauce is the consistency of double/heavy cream.

Once the pasta is cooked, drain it, then immediately add it to the pan with the sauce. Turn the pasta several times to coat it with sauce, add the grated Parmesan and stir well.

Serve simply in bowls with some ripped basil sprinkled over the top.

Tabbouleh

PREPARE: **20 MINUTES** COOK: **5 MINUTES** SERVES: **4**

I've replaced the traditional bulgur wheat in this recipe with pearl barley, which give a delicious nuttiness of flavour and turns this salad from a side dish into a hearty meal. The Middle Eastern spiced tomatoes are the star of the show and make this a spectacular dish.

100 g/½ cup pearl barley

500 ml/2 cups vegetable stock

grated zest of 1 lemon

a small bunch of fresh mint

2 large bunches of fresh flat-leaf parsley

300 g/11 oz. firm tomatoes, finely chopped

freshly squeezed juice of 2 lemons

1 teaspoon white wine vinegar

a pinch of freshly ground black pepper

a pinch of ground allspice

a pinch of ground coriander

a pinch of ground cinnamon

extra virgin olive oil, to drizzle

table salt, to season

1 crusty sourdough loaf, sliced, or flatbreads, to serve

Put the barley in a large saucepan, cover with the stock and add a generous pinch of salt. Bring to the boil, then immediately take off the heat, add the lemon zest and leave to cool. The barley should absorb all of the liquid and be firm but not hard.

Leaving a handful of the mint and parsley leaves for dressing the dish, finely chop the parsley leaves and stems and the mint leaves. Add them to the cooled barley and stir through.

Put the tomatoes in a separate bowl and add the lemon juice and white wine vinegar. Add the black pepper, allspice, coriander and cinnamon, and toss to combine. Taste the salad and add a little more of the spices if you prefer it more heavily spiced.

To serve, spoon the pearl barley onto plates, then the tomatoes. Sprinkle with the reserved mint and parsley leaves and drizzle a good glug of olive oil over the top. Enjoy with slices of crusty sourdough or flatbreads.

Goat's cheese and marjoram ravioli marinara

PREPARE: **30 MINUTES** COOK: **10 MINUTES** SERVES: **4**

The marinara or mariners' sauce is simple and balances well with the salty goat's cheese and fragrant marjoram of the ravioli. Wonton wrappers make a brilliant cheat's ravioli pasta and can be found in the freezer in Asian supermarkets. You can prepare the ravioli up to three days ahead.

250 g/9 oz. soft goat's cheese

a large bunch of fresh marjoram

32 x 10-cm/4-inch square wonton wrappers

2 eggs, beaten

grated Parmesan cheese, to serve

table salt, to season

MARINARA SAUCE

2 garlic cloves, crushed

50 ml/3½ tablespoons extra virgin olive oil

400 g/2 cups canned chopped tomatoes

200 ml/¾ cup vegetable stock

2 teaspoons capers

Put the goat's cheese, two-thirds of the chopped marjoram leaves and a pinch of salt in a large mixing bowl and stir together.

Lay half of the wonton wrappers on a clean work surface and paint the edges with beaten egg. Spoon 1 tablespoon of the cheese mixture in the middle of each egg-washed wrapper, then lay the other half of the wonton wrappers on top. Gently press together to remove any air. Leave the ravioli to dry for 10 minutes or so. If you're making them in advance, put them in an airtight container, using baking parchment between each ravioli to stop them sticking.

To make the marinara sauce, put the garlic and olive oil in a saucepan over a medium heat. Cook until the garlic is just starting to brown, then add the chopped tomatoes, stock and capers, and bring to a low simmer.

Bring a large pan of salted water to a rolling boil, then gently add the ravioli. Maintain a low simmer for 3 minutes, then carefully remove the ravioli and place four on each serving plate. Spoon over the marinara sauce, decorate with a few marjoram leaves and sprinkle with Parmesan cheese.

Spaghetti puttanesca

PREPARE: **5 MINUTES** COOK: **20 MINUTES** SERVES: **4**

The wonderful spicy and salty combination of capers, chillies/chiles and olives make this the perfect dish to eat outside on a warm summer's evening.

300 g/11 oz. bronze-dyed dried spaghetti

extra virgin olive oil, for frying

4 garlic cloves, crushed

150 g/½ cup concentrated tomato purée/paste

1 teaspoon dried chilli/hot red pepper flakes

2 teaspoons capers

200 ml/¾ cup vegetable stock

200 ml/¾ cup red wine

100 g/1 cup pitted black olives, roughly chopped

100 g/1⅓ cups grated Parmesan cheese, plus extra to serve

Half fill a large saucepan with water and bring to a rolling boil. Add a couple of teaspoons of table salt then the pasta. Leave on a rolling boil for 1 minute less than the cooking time listed on the packet instructions.

Just cover the base of a large saucepan with olive oil and set over a medium heat. Add the garlic and cook for a couple of minutes until it starts to colour. Add the tomato purée/paste, dried chilli/hot red pepper flakes and capers, and cook through for 2–3 minutes. Slowly add the stock, stirring to combine, then add the wine and simmer for 5 minutes to cook off the alcohol.

Once the pasta is cooked, drain, then immediately add to the pan with the sauce. Turn the pasta several times to coat it with sauce. Add the 50 g/½ cup of the olives and the grated Parmesan.

Serve immediately, topped with extra Parmesan and the remaining olives.

Tomato tacos with guacamole

PREPARE: **20 MINUTES** SERVES: **4**

Spicy, hot and sour. There is a wonderful balance between the crunch of the tacos, the smoothness of the guacamole and sour cream, and heat of the chilli/chile to this dish.

300 g/2 cups cherry tomatoes, quartered

a small bunch of fresh coriander/cilantro, finely chopped

grated zest of 1 lime

2 teaspoons white wine vinegar

2 jalapeño chillies/chiles, thinly sliced

1–2 teaspoons cayenne pepper, to season, plus extra to serve

sea salt, to season

GUACAMOLE

2 large avocados

freshly squeezed juice of 1 lime

a small bunch of fresh coriander/cilantro, roughly chopped

1 garlic clove, crushed

1 red onion, finely diced

TO SERVE

8 taco shells

sour cream

To make the tomato salad, mix all the ingredients together in a large mixing bowl, adding cayenne pepper to taste; just 1 teaspoon of cayenne pepper makes a nice, moderately hot salad. Finish with a generous pinch of sea salt.

To make the guacamole, cut the avocados in half using a small, sharp knife. Remove the pit, scoop out the flesh and roughly chop. Mix in the lime juice immediately to stop it discolouring. Add the coriander/cilantro, garlic and onion, mix all the ingredients together and mash a little using a fork to achieve a rough texture.

Serve the salad with the guacamole at the table, with taco shells and sour cream on the side, or build the tacos by putting a large spoonful of the tomato salad in each one, then a similar amount of the guacamole on top. Finish with a dollop of sour cream and a sprinkle of cayenne pepper.

Panzanella-stuffed tomatoes

PREPARE: **25 MINUTES** COOK: **20 MINUTES** SERVES: **4**

Although a classic Italian dish, the stuffed tomato, to me, is more reminiscent of 1980s dinner parties and raises a smile every time it is served. I've made this recipe as a version of an Italian tomato panzanella salad, which I think benefits from a little cooking to release the flavours.

4 large or beef tomatoes

200 g/3½ cups cubed stale sourdough bread

1 small brown onion, sliced into thin wedges

2 celery sticks, sliced

1 garlic clove, crushed

1 cucumber, peeled, quartered and cut into small triangles

a small bunch of fresh basil leaves, finely chopped

2 tablespoons balsamic vinegar

50 g/⅔ cup grated Parmesan cheese

olive oil, for frying

sea salt and freshly ground black pepper, to season

mixed salad leaves, to serve (optional)

Slice a thin piece from the base of the tomatoes so they sit upright unaided. Slice about 1.5 cm/⅝ inch from the top of the tomatoes, discard these slices or reserve to bake as a cook's treat. Carefully scoop out the tomato seeds and flesh and put in a bowl. Crush the seeds and flesh with the back of a fork to a coarse pulp.

Cover the base of a frying pan/skillet with olive oil and set over a medium heat. Once the oil sizzles when a cube of bread is dropped into the pan, add the rest of the bread and fry for 2–3 minutes, carefully tossing the bread cubes repeatedly to coat with oil and crisp up. Reduce the heat, then add the onion wedges, celery and crushed garlic and reduce the heat to cook over a low heat, tossing occasionally till the onions and celery have become translucent.

Preheat the oven to 180°C (350°F) Gas 4.

When ready to serve (no sooner or the bread will go soggy), mix the cooked ingredients with the tomato pulp, cucumber and basil. Season with a generous pinch of salt and the balsamic vinegar.

Stuff the tomatoes with the mixture and arrange on a baking sheet. Lightly cover with grated Parmesan and a little black pepper.

Bake in the preheated oven for 15 minutes and serve immediately as an appetizer or with mixed salad leaves for a main meal.

Aubergine lasagne

PREPARE: **30 MINUTES** COOK: **40 MINUTES** SERVES: **4**

I love using aubergine/eggplant in a ragù; it gives a sweet, savoury depth of flavour that leaves me wanting more. Why not make double the ragù mixture and use it as a great spaghetti sauce the following day?

2 large aubergines/eggplants, peeled and diced into 5-mm/¼-inch pieces

100 g/7 tablespoons butter

4 garlic cloves, crushed

6 shallots, finely diced

400 g/2 cups canned chopped tomatoes

a small bunch of fresh marjoram

15 sheets dried egg lasagna

table salt, to season

mixed salad leaves or fries, to serve

CHEESE SAUCE

30 g/2 tablespoons butter

30 g/2 tablespoons plain/all-purpose flour

500 ml/2 cups whole milk

100 g/1 cup plus 2 tablespoons grated strong Cheddar cheese

100 g/1 cup minus 2 tablespoons grated Gruyère cheese

50 g/⅔ cup grated Parmesan cheese

120 g/4 oz. mozzarella cheese, thinly sliced

a 22 x 30-cm/9 x 12-inch casserole dish

Preheat the oven to 160°C (325°F) Gas 3.

To make the ragù, put the aubergine/eggplant in a large mixing bowl and dust with table salt. Leave for 30 minutes, to draw out the liquid.

Put the butter in a large, heavy-based saucepan and set over a medium heat, until the butter is sizzling.

Quickly rinse the aubergine/eggplant pieces under running water, then add them to the saucepan along with the garlic and shallots. Cook for 20 minutes, stirring regularly, until the mixture is cooked through and just starting to turn golden. Add the tomatoes, a good pinch of table salt, a handful of ripped marjoram leaves and stir to combine. Take the saucepan off the heat and set aside while you make the cheese sauce.

To make the cheese sauce, begin by making a roux. Put the butter and flour in a dry saucepan and set over a medium heat until the mixture forms crumbs and is just starting to colour. Slowly, add about 125 ml/½ cup of milk and whisk to combine into a smooth, thick paste. With the pan still on the heat, keep adding the milk, 125 ml/½ cup at a time, and whisk together to combine until all of the milk has been added to the sauce and it is thin and smooth.

Reduce to a low heat and add two-thirds of the Cheddar, Gruyère and Parmesan cheeses to the sauce. Whisk gently until the sauce is smooth, then add the mozzarella cheese. Whisk until the cheese has melted and you have a smooth sauce.

Spread a layer of the ragù into the bottom of the casserole dish, then a layer of lasagne sheets. Follow with a layer of cheese sauce and another layer of lasagne sheets. Repeat three times, finishing with a cheese sauce layer.

Top the cheese sauce layer with the excess cheese and bake in the preheated oven for 40 minutes.

Serve with salad, or, if you're feeling extra hungry, fries, too.

Jambalaya

PREPARE: **15 MINUTES** COOK: **25 MINUTES** SERVES: **4**

Jambalaya may have its origins in Spanish paella, but here, I have added heat with chilli/chile and smoke with paprika. I like to roast the okra and broccoli, which gives it a wonderful nutty flavour and a crisp texture.

1 green (bell) pepper, deseeded and finely diced

1 red (bell) pepper, deseeded and finely diced

4 sticks celery, thinly sliced

2 onions, finely diced

2 teaspoons smoked paprika

2 red chillies/chiles, thinly sliced

500 g/4½ cups paella rice

1 litre/quart vegetable stock

100 g/½ cup frozen peas

50 g/⅓ cup frozen sweetcorn

100 g/3½ oz. fresh okra, trimmed and halved lengthways

100 g/3½ oz. broccoli florets

100 g/1 heaped cup mangetout/snow peas or sugarsnap beans, trimmed

4 tomatoes, cut into eight pieces

vegetable oil, for frying

table salt, to season

Preheat the oven to 180°C (350°F) Gas 4.

In a large saucepan, cover the base with vegetable oil and bring to a moderate temperature over a medium heat. Add the (bell) peppers, celery, onions and smoked paprika and allow them to cook for a few minutes, stirring regularly, until the vegetables are starting to turn golden and catch on the base of the pan. Add the chillies/chiles, then the rice and stir to just coat the rice with the oil. Now add the stock and a level teaspoon of table salt and bring to a low simmer. Continue to simmer for 10 minutes.

Add the frozen peas and sweetcorn, and bring back to a simmer. Continue to simmer for another 5 minutes, until the rice is cooked.

While the rice is cooking, put the okra and broccoli on a baking sheet, drizzle with oil and add a good sprinkle of salt. Toss to coat evenly, then roast them in the preheated oven for 10 minutes.

Once the rice is cooked, add the mangetout/snow peas or sugarsnap beans and tomatoes, and stir through.

Spoon the rice onto warm plates and place the roasted okra and broccoli on top to finish the jambalaya.

Braised red cabbage and burnt aubergine babaganoush

PREPARE: **20 MINUTES** COOK: **45 MINUTES** SERVES: **4**

The babaganoush and red cabbage in this Middle Eastern-inspired dish can be made individually as delicious side dishes or served together for a larger vegetarian meal.

1/2 red cabbage, core removed and thinly sliced

200 ml/3/4 cup red wine

50 g/1/4 cup dark brown sugar

50 ml/31/2 tablespoons balsamic vinegar

2 aubergines/eggplants

1 onion, roughly chopped

2 garlic cloves, crushed

2 tomatoes, cut into 8 pieces

8 pitta breads, quartered

a small bunch of fresh flat-leaf parsley, chopped

olive oil, for frying, plus extra to serve

table salt, to season

Put the cabbage in a small saucepan with the wine, brown sugar and balsamic vinegar. Cover, set over a medium heat and bring to a low simmer for 20 minutes. Remove the lid and continue to simmer for a further 20–30 minutes. Stir regularly, until the cooking liquor has thickened and reduced to just 5 mm/1/4 inch deep in the bottom of the pan. Leave to cool.

Trim a thin slice from each side of one of the aubergines/eggplants, then slice into four long strips. Cover the base of a frying pan/skillet with 3 mm/1/8 inch of olive oil and set over a medium heat until the oil starts to shimmer. Put the aubergine/eggplant strips in the pan and leave until they are golden. Turn and cook on the other side. Once cooked, drain on paper towels to mop up any excess oil.

Preheat the oven to 180°C (350°F) Gas 4.

To make the babaganoush, preheat a heavy-based frying pan/skillet with no oil in it over a medium heat, until it feels hot when you hold your hand about 15 cm/6 inches above the surface. Peel the other aubergine/eggplant and slice it into 5-mm/1/4-inch strips. Lightly oil, then carefully place the strips in the hot frying pan/skillet and leave until they start to blacken. Turn and blacken the other side. Remove the pan from the heat and transfer the aubergine/eggplant strips to a large mixing bowl.

Using the remaining oil in the frying pan/skillet used to blacken the aubergine/eggplant, fry the onion, garlic and tomatoes over a low heat for about 15 minutes, until the onion is translucent; add a little more oil if needed.

Add the onion, garlic and tomatoes to the blackened aubergine strips in the mixing bowl. Purée them using a handheld electric blender until nearly smooth. Add a pinch of salt to taste and set aside.

To finish, arrange the reserved cooked aubergine/eggplant slices on a baking sheet. Arrange the pitta quarters on another baking sheet and heat both in the preheated oven for 10 minutes. Place a hot aubergine/eggplant slice on each plate with a generous covering of babaganoush and red cabbage. Finish with a sprinkling of parsley. Place the pitta bread on the side of the plates with a small pot of olive oil for dipping.

Bulbs and alliums

ONIONS • SHALLOTS • GARLIC • WILD GARLIC/RAMPS
FENNEL • LEEKS

My first restaurant was called The Wild Garlic, so it's no surprise that I love the rich, earthy flavour of garlic and onions. They provide the aromatic depth and savoury base flavours to so many dishes. I enjoy foraging for wild plants and use fennel, garlic and dandelions in this chapter. My Wild Garlic and Nettle Soup on page 72 is great fun – you can take the children out to forage for a few ingredients, then come home and cook them into a delicious soup together. Make sure you know exactly what you are picking; if you're not 100% sure, ask someone who is.

Cooking onions and garlic is easy, remember their flavour will improve the longer you cook them. Slow-roasted garlic is such a great ingredient. I use it on toast with some strong cheese and Szechuan pepper on page 76. This recipe also works well with my vegan Dairy-free Cheese recipe on page 9. You could use slow-roasted garlic in the French Onion Soup on page 71 for a richer flavour, or stick with the crushed garlic for a lighter bowl. The Red Onion Tarte Tatin with Goat's Cheese and Dandelion Sauce on page 68 is really simple but has become a restaurant favourite for many customers because of its delicious, smooth taste. The hint of bitterness in the sauce from the dandelion leaves balances the rich onion flavours perfectly.

Fennel can be the star of the show. Don't be scared of the strength of its flavour when raw. When poached or slow-roasted, it becomes much more rounded in flavour and balances other vegetables well. The Fennel and Roast Tomato Lasagne on page 80 is my wife's favourite meal.

Red onion tarte tatin with goat's cheese and dandelion sauce

PREPARE: **40 MINUTES** COOK: **20 MINUTES** SERVES: **4**

One of the most popular dishes on my restaurant menu, this red onion tarte tatin is delicious and attractive to look at. The dandelion leaves add a wonderful bitterness to the cheese sauce that balances the flavours perfectly.

2 large red onions

250 g/9 oz. readymade puff pastry

50 g/3$\frac{1}{2}$ tablespoons butter

4 tablespoons caster/granulated sugar

1 egg, beaten

100 ml/$\frac{1}{3}$ cup double/heavy cream

100 g/3$\frac{1}{2}$ oz. goat's cheese

1 tablespoon sour cream

7 dandelion leaves, finely chopped, plus flowers to decorate

table salt, to season

a small bag of washed salad leaves, to serve

Peel then put the whole onions in a saucepan of water, set over a medium heat and bring to a low simmer for 15 minutes. Remove the pan from the heat and leave the onions in the water to soak for a further 15 minutes.

Preheat the oven to 180°C (350°F) Gas 4.

Carefully lift the onions from the saucepan using a slotted spoon and set aside to cool completely before carefully slicing in half across the middle.

Roll out the puff pastry to a thickness of about 2 mm/$\frac{1}{8}$ inch on a lightly floured surface. Cut four rounds, large enough to cover the onion halves, using a small, sharp knife to create a clean edge otherwise the pastry will not rise at the edges.

Put the onion halves cut-side down on a chopping board. Place a thin slice of butter and $\frac{1}{2}$ teaspoon of sugar on top of each half, then cover with a round of puff pastry. Glaze with the beaten egg and set aside.

In an ovenproof frying pan/skillet, cover the base with the remaining sugar and a little water, and heat this mixture until it is just starting to foam.

Carefully, with a fish slice, transfer the onion tarts, still cut-side down, to the pan and cook for a few minutes until lightly caramelized.

Put the pan in the preheated oven and bake for 15–20 minutes, until the pastry has risen and is golden brown.

Meanwhile, prepare the sauce. Put the double/heavy cream and goat's cheese in a saucepan set over a medium–high heat until just bubbling. Take the saucepan off the heat, add the sour cream then whisk to combine all the ingredients. Add the dandelion leaves and a pinch of salt, taste and adjust the seasoning as necessary.

To serve, lay the tarts on a bed of salad leaves pastry-side down. Pour some cheese sauce over the top, or serve on the side if preferred, and decorate with dandelion flower petals.

French onion soup

PREPARE: **20 MINUTES** COOK: **1 HOUR** SERVES: **4**

A rich, sweet, onion soup, that has a taste like nothing else I know. Best served with mini cheese on toasts for a tangy punch against the silky smooth broth.

2 litres/quarts vegetable stock

100 g/7 tablespoons butter

1 kg/2 lbs. large onions, peeled and thinly sliced

6 garlic cloves, crushed

250 ml/1 cup red wine

50 ml/3½ tablespoons sherry vinegar

50 g/scant ½ cup plain/all-purpose flour

8 slices French baguette

250 g/2½ packed cups grated strong Cheddar cheese

table salt and freshly ground black pepper, to season

Pour the stock into a saucepan and set over a high heat. Simmer until it is reduced by half to intensify the flavour.

Melt the butter in a separate large saucepan over a medium heat. Add the onions, sprinkling 2 teaspoons of table salt over them and stirring to combine. Cook until the onions become glassy and are just starting to caramelize and catch on the bottom of the pan.

Add the crushed garlic, then the wine and vinegar, and continue to cook on a low heat, stirring occasionally, until they are reduced and the bottom remains clean when the stirring spoon is dragged across it.

Sprinkle the flour over the cooked onions and garlic and stir to combine.

Add the stock and bring to a low simmer. Leave to simmer on a very low heat for about 30 minutes before tasting; add a pinch or two of table salt, if needed.

Preheat the oven to 180°C (350°F) Gas 4.

Lay the baguette slices on a baking sheet and bake in the preheated oven for 5 minutes until they are starting to crisp and brown. Sprinkle about 150 g/1½ cups of the cheese over them and return to the oven for another 5 minutes to melt the cheese to a golden colour.

Put a little cheese in the base of four large serving bowls, then ladle the onion soup over the top. Place two cheesy toasts on top of each portion straight from the oven and serve sprinkled with black pepper.

Wild garlic and nettle soup with a poached egg

PREPARE: **5 MINUTES** COOK: **60 MINUTES** SERVES: **4**

Nettles and wild garlic/ramps are a traditional spring combination and they make a delicious soup. Use an old pair of gloves when picking nettles to protect your hands but don't worry about eating them, 30 seconds in boiling water is all it takes to remove the sting.

4 carrots, peeled and finely diced

2 onions, finely diced

2 celery sticks, sliced

leaves of 2–3 large bunches of wild nettles (available in health food stores, at farmers' markets or online, see Note)

12 wild garlic/ramp leaves

4 eggs

150 g/1¼ cup grated Gruyère cheese

table salt freshly ground black pepper, to season

Put the carrots, onions and celery in a large pot with 2 litres/quarts of water. Set over a medium heat and bring to a low simmer for 30 minutes. Add the nettle and wild garlic/ramp leaves and continue to simmer for a further 20 minutes.

Purée the soup using a handheld electric blender to form a smooth liquid. Keep warm.

In a separate pan, cook the poached eggs. First, place the whole egg (shell on) in a saucepan of simmering water for 10 seconds, then plunge it in a bowl of cold water until it's cool enough to touch. Add a few drops of vinegar to the pan of simmering water, then crack in the eggs. You may need to do this in batches depending on the size of your pan. Cook the eggs for 3 minutes each then lift from the water using a slotted spoon. Carefully lay the eggs on paper towels to drain off any excess water.

Preheat the grill/broiler to hot.

Ladle the soup into warm bowls. Gently, place a poached egg on top of the soup and sprinkle the Gruyère cheese over. Set the bowls under the hot grill/broiler until the cheese is golden. Serve immediately sprinkled with black pepper.

Note: Wild nettles can be foraged from clean, unsplayed areas but can also be bought in garden centres or online from retailers such as Farmdrop in the UK and Marx Foods in the US. If you really get a taste for nettle, you might consider planting them in your garden or window box.

Take care to wear protective gloves when handling nettles before they are cooked to avoid being stung.

Shallot and fennel quiches

PREPARE: **45 MINUTES** COOK: **20 MINUTES** SERVES: **4**

Delicious served hot, straight from the oven, or cold as part of a picnic spread with a glass of cider or crisp Chardonnay.

2 banana shallots, halved lengthways

1 fennel bulb, diced into 5-mm/¼-inch pieces

150 g/1 stick plus 2 tablespoons butter

1 egg

200 g/1½ cups plain/all-purpose flour

1 egg white, whisked, to glaze

vegetable oil, to drizzle

table salt and freshly ground black pepper, to season

CUSTARD

150 ml/⅔ cup double/heavy cream

150 ml/⅔ cup whole milk

1 egg yolk

4 eggs

4 x 15-cm/6-inch fluted tart pans

Preheat the oven to 180°C (350°F) Gas 4.

Drizzle the shallot halves and fennel with vegetable oil and sprinkle with a big pinch of table salt.

Put the shallots and fennel on a baking sheet and bake in the preheated oven for 15 minutes. Remove from the oven but leave the heat on.

To make the pastry, freeze the butter for a couple of hours, then grate with a cheese grater. Mix the butter, egg, flour and a large pinch of salt in a bowl using a fork to achieve the consistency of fine breadcrumbs. Squeeze the mixture together to form a ball of dough, wrap it in clingfilm/plastic wrap and chill in the fridge for 30 minutes.

Remove the pastry from the fridge and roll out on a cool, lightly floured surface to a thickness of about 3 mm/⅛ inch. Use a sharp knife to cut out rounds that are slightly larger than the tart pans and press gently into each pan. Prick the bases with a fork and bake in the still-warm oven for 10 minutes.

Remove from the oven, glaze with the whisked egg white and sprinkle with a pinch of table salt. Return to the oven for 2 minutes. Remove and allow to cool. Keep the heat on.

Place a shallot half in each tart and a tablespoon each of the roasted fennel.

To make the custard, whisk all the ingredients together and pour into the tart cases until they are nearly full.

Bake the tarts in the still-warm oven for 15–20 minutes until the custard is set. Remove and either serve immediately with a sprinkle of cracked black pepper, or cool and keep in the fridge to eat them cold with a simple salad.

Slow-roasted garlic, cheese and Szechuan peppercorn toasts

PREPARE: **5 MINUTES (PLUS ROASTING TIME)** COOK: **5 MINUTES** SERVES: **4**

When I'm cooking the Sunday roast, I often put a whole bulb of garlic wrapped in foil in the oven, too. This adds lovely aromas to the roast but, even better, provides a wonderful savoury ingredient for all sorts of dishes during the week. The garlic cooks in its own juices and can be stored in the fridge for several days; a roast garlic paste can be squeezed from each clove. I add it to soups, pasta sauces and, if I don't have to see anyone for a few hours, I put it on toast with cheese and peppercorns, as in this recipe. Szechuan peppercorns can be found with dried herbs and spices in the supermarket and make a great alternative to black peppercorns.

1 garlic bulb

4 slices sourdough

salted butter, to spread

50 g/¹/₂ cup grated strong Cheddar cheese

50 g/²/₃ cup grated Parmesan cheese

whole dried Szechuan peppercorns

stout, to serve

Preheat the oven to 180°C (350°F) Gas 4.

Put the whole bulb of garlic on a baking sheet and cook in the preheated oven for 45 minutes. You can easily do this while you're cooking something else and save it in the fridge until you need it. You will now have a bulb of soft garlic paste that can be squeezed, like a tube of toothpaste, one clove at a time.

Preheat a grill/broiler to medium.

Lightly toast and butter the sourdough slices.

Carefully squeeze 1–3 garlic cloves onto each toast; spread the garlic evenly and place them on a baking sheet.

Sprinkle the grated cheeses over the top of the toasts.

Crush or grind the peppercorns lightly using a pestle and mortar or pepper grinder and sprinkle over the toasts.

Put the toasts under the preheated grill/broiler for a few minutes until the cheese is bubbling and starting to brown. Keep your eye on them as they can turn quickly.

Serve immediately, accompanied by a glass of stout.

Coddled eggs with creamed leeks

PREPARE: **10 MINUTES** COOK: **35 MINUTES** SERVES: **4**

A coddled egg is comfort food at its very best. This recipe combines the traditional baked egg with delicious, sweet and savoury leeks, for a remarkably filling and tasty meal. Use duck eggs if you can get them for a richer flavour, but the recipe works well with free-range hen's eggs, too.

2 large leeks, whites thinly sliced into rings

150 g/1 stick plus 2 tablespoons butter

75 g/1 cup grated Parmesan cheese

75 g/³/4 cup grated Cheddar cheese

150 ml/²/3 cup double/heavy cream

4 duck or hen's eggs

Tabasco sauce, to taste

table salt, to season

Preheat the oven to 160°C (325°F) Gas 3.

Put the sliced leeks and butter into a large saucepan set over a low heat. Add a couple of generous pinches of table salt.

Once the butter has melted, stir the mixture and cover with a lid. Leave on a low heat for 15–20 minutes, stirring every few minutes until the mixture is creamy and tender.

Put the cheeses in a mixing bowl with the cream and a good pinch of salt. Stir gently to combine.

Spoon the creamed leeks into four large ramekins. Next, crack an egg on top of the leeks in each ramekin. Carefully sprinkle the cheese mixture on top of the egg until it is covered. Finally, add a few drops of Tabasco to each ramekin.

Cook in the preheated oven for 20 minutes. The cheese top should be just starting to turn golden after this time.

Remove from the oven and serve immediately.

Fennel and roast tomato lasagne with sweet potato chips

PREPARE: **60 MINUTES** COOK: **40 MINUTES** SERVES: **4**

This is a dish that my children love and would choose over a traditional beef lasagne every time.

3 fennel bulbs, thinly sliced

800 g/1¾ lbs. tomatoes on the vine

2 tablespoons balsamic vinegar

300 ml/1¼ cups double/heavy cream

100 g/1⅓ cups grated Parmesan cheese

1 packet of good-quality dried lasagne pasta

table salt and freshly ground black pepper, to season

Sweet Potato Chips (page 96), to serve

Preheat the oven to 180°C (350°F) Gas 4.

Spread the sliced fennel out on a roasting pan, drizzle with olive oil and sprinkle with a pinch of salt and pepper.

Put the tomatoes (still on the vine) on a separate baking sheet, drizzle with olive oil and season with the balsamic vinegar and a pinch of salt and pepper.

Put both sheets in the preheated oven and cook for 30 minutes.

Remove the fennel, pour over the cream, mix with the fennel, and return to the oven for a further 10 minutes.

Transfer the tomatoes to a large mixing bowl. Carefully remove the vine and lightly crush the tomatoes with the back of a fork. Leave the oven on.

Add most of the cheese to the fennel and cream mixture and stir, making a thick cheesy sauce with a custard-like consistency.

In a deep casserole dish, start to assemble the lasagne with a thin layer of tomatoes, then a layer of lasagne sheets, followed by a layer of fennel and another layer of lasagne sheets. Continue with this pattern of layers; tomatoes, pasta, fennel, pasta, finishing with fennel, onto which you can sprinkle the remaining cheese. Cover with foil and set aside.

Remove the foil from the lasagne for the last 10 minutes of cooking to allow the top to brown.

Remove from the oven, cut into slices and serve with sweet potato chips.

Pan-fried fennel and dandelion with a fried egg

PREPARE: **10 MINUTES** COOK: **15 MINUTES** SERVES: **4**

The strong flavours of fennel and dandelion balance each other really well, making for an unusual, light and tasty meal.

2 teaspoons sesame oil

2 garlic cloves, crushed

1 fennel bulb and fronds, thinly sliced

100 g/2 cups dandelion leaves (available in health food stores, at farmers' markets or online)

1–2 splashes of balsamic vinegar

1/2 iceberg lettuce, thinly sliced

4 eggs

vegetable oil, for frying

sea salt and freshly ground black pepper, to season

In a large frying pan/skillet, pour the sesame oil, then add enough vegetable oil to thinly coat the base of the pan.

Set over a medium heat and add the garlic, then the sliced fennel and a generous pinch of salt. Cook for about 5 minutes, turning constantly, until the garlic and fennel are starting to turn a golden colour.

Add the dandelion leaves and a splash of balsamic vinegar and continue to cook on a low heat for another 5 minutes. Add the lettuce and another splash of balsamic vinegar. Cook for a final few minutes until the lettuce leaves are warmed through.

To serve, spoon the greens onto warm plates and keep warm.

Return the frying pan/skillet to the heat and turn it up. Crack four eggs into the pan, cook for 1 minute to colour the bottom of the eggs, then cover and cook for another 1 minute.

Carefully lift the eggs on top of the greens. Add a good pinch of salt and pepper and decorate with fennel fronds.

Fennel, watercress, red onion and thyme gratin

PREPARE: **15 MINUTES** COOK: **45 MINUTES** SERVES: **4**

Fennel can be intense in flavour, so I boil it for a while to remove the harshness that often puts people off. What remains is a delicious, savoury flavour, that is well balanced when paired with sweet red onions and hot watercress.

2 fennel bulbs, thinly sliced

4 large red onions, thinly sliced

leaves of a bunch of fresh thyme

100 g/2 cups watercress leaves

500 ml/2 cups double/heavy cream

3 slices bread

50 g/²/₃ cup grated Parmesan cheese

table salt, to season

Preheat the oven to 160°C (325°F) Gas 3.

Put the fennel in a saucepan, cover with water, add a little salt and bring to a simmer over a medium heat. Continue to simmer for 10 minutes, then drain.

Add the red onion, thyme and watercress to the pan of boiled fennel and mix together. Spoon the greens into four individual ovenproof dishes, just cover with cream and a light sprinkling of salt.

Bake in the preheated oven for 20 minutes.

Put the bread, cheese and a generous pinch of salt into a food processor and blitz to a fine crumb.

Remove the dishes from the oven and sprinkle with the breadcrumbs.

Increase the oven to 180°C (350°F) Gas 4 and return the dishes to the oven for a further 10 minutes, until the tops are golden.

Serve warm from the oven.

Potatoes, squash and corn

POTATOES • SWEET POTATOES • BUTTERNUT SQUASH
PUMPKIN • COURGETTES/ZUCCHINI • CORN

This chapter is all about the flavours of comfort and familiarity. Sweetcorn, for me, is one of the flavours of my childhood; we used to grow it in our family garden and the taste of corn, simply boiled, or even raw straight from the plant, always transports me straight back there. I remember the joy of eating hot sweetcorn with oodles of butter dripping from my chin, as I scoffed cob after cob, ear after ear.

The Sweetcorn Fritters on page 100 are a simple way to make a cheap but delicious meal for the children, even better, roasted corn in the husk then rolled in brown butter and soy (also page 100) is an explosion of flavour you won't be able to get enough of.

Potato Dauphinoise on page 95 takes potatoes to a new level. Sliced and pan-fried in butter, with a little cheese on top, it is about as good as it gets in terms of comfort food. While the Croquettes on the same page are the perfect way to use up leftover mashed potatoes and are delicious with a good dollop of tomato ketchup.

Pumpkins, sweet potatoes and squash all add a sweet and savoury flavour that balances well with salty flavours like miso and cheese. The Roast Butternut Squash and Four Cheese Salad and Sweet Potato and Miso Soup with Seaweed on page 88 are simple to make and satisfying to eat. And, best of all, both are easy to make and can be prepared in advance.

Roast butternut squash and four cheese salad

PREPARE: **20 MINUTES** COOK: **15 MINUTES** SERVES: **4**

You can serve the butternut squash and hazelnuts made in this recipe hot or cold; I prefer to enjoy them hot, straight from the oven for a rich and intense flavour.

1 butternut squash, peeled and diced into 2-cm/³/4-inch pieces

vegetable oil, to coat

150 g/1 cup peeled hazelnuts

200 g/7 oz. Cheddar cheese, diced into 5-mm/¹/4-inch pieces

150 g/5¹/2 oz. blue cheese, crumbled

120 g/4 oz. mozzarella cheese, sliced into bite-sized pieces

50 ml/3¹/2 tablespoons General Purpose Vinaigrette (page 171)

100 g/1¹/3 cups grated Parmesan cheese

12 dandelion leaves (available in health food stores, at farmers' markets or online), finely chopped

70 g/3 cups rocket/arugula

70 g/3 cups mixed lettuce leaves

table salt, to season

Preheat the oven to 180°C (350°F) Gas 4.

Toss the butternut squash in some vegetable oil with the hazelnuts and a generous pinch of table salt. Transfer to a baking sheet and bake in the preheated oven for 10–15 minutes, or until the butternut squash has softened and the hazelnuts are starting to brown.

Put the Cheddar, blue cheese and mozzarella into a large mixing bowl, add the vinaigrette, sprinkle the Parmesan over the top and toss to combine.

Add the dandelion leaves to the cheese mixture and stir gently. Add the rocket/arugula and lettuce leaves and gently toss the salad to combine the cheeses and leaves together. The leaves should have a light coating of the vinaigrette but add more if you prefer.

Lay the salad on four plates and sprinkle the baked butternut squash and hazelnuts over the top to serve.

Sweet potato and miso soup with seaweed

PREPARE: **5 MINUTES** COOK: **20 MINUTES** SERVES: **4**

I use a sweet potato and miso paste in the restaurant all the time, the perfect marriage, it's one of those unidentifiable flavour combinations that keeps customers coming back. This soup is rich with salty, savoury and sweet elements combining to give a remarkable depth of flavour.

20 g/1 cup dried mixed seaweed

70 g/4¹/2 tablespoons yellow miso paste

4 sweet potatoes, peeled and roughly diced

100 ml/¹/3 cup double/heavy cream

table salt, to season

Put the seaweed in a large mixing bowl and cover with boiling water, add 20 g/1¹/4 tablespoons of the miso paste and a pinch of table salt. Stir, then leave for 20 minutes for the seaweed to rehydrate.

Put the sweet potatoes into a saucepan with the remaining miso paste and just cover with cold water. Cover and bring to a low simmer over a medium heat. Simmer for 15 minutes. Check the sweet potatoes with a knife – they should be soft and cooked through. Simmer for another 5 minutes if needed.

Remove the pan from the heat and, using a handheld electric blender, purée the miso broth and sweet potato to a smooth consistency. Add the cream and a pinch of salt, and blend to combine.

Drain the rehydrated seaweed. Pour the soup into bowls and decorate with the seaweed to serve.

Pumpkin pie

PREPARE: **20 MINUTES** COOK: **40 MINUTES** SERVES: **4**

This is a beautiful autumn/fall dish. It has the lovely sweetness and savoury flavours of roast pumpkin and spices with a peppery rocket/arugula salad to finish.

300 g/3 cups cubed pumpkin flesh

1/2 teaspoon ground allspice

1/2 teaspoon ground ginger

1 teaspoon ground cinnamon

2 eggs

50 g/3¹/₂ tablespoons strong honey

12 sheets filo/Phyllo pastry

1 beaten egg white, to glaze

50 g/1 cup fresh rocket/arugula leaves

mustard oil, to serve

4 x 10-cm/4-inch diameter metal baking rings

baking beans

Put the pumpkin into a saucepan and cover with water.

The next day, bring to the boil over a medium heat and cook for 10 minutes until soft. Drain off the water using a sieve/strainer and suspend the pumpkin pieces over the pan to thoroughly drain and dry out for 30 minutes. Place the pumpkin pieces in a food processor and purée them together with the allspice, ginger, cinnamon, whole eggs and honey until smooth.

Preheat the oven to 160°C (325°F) Gas 3.

Cut the filo/Phyllo pastry sheets in half, then line the baking rings with six layers of filo/Phyllo pastry each – stagger them and let them hang over the sides. Brush each layer of pastry with the beaten egg white as you place them in the baking rings.

Put a handful of baking beans onto 4 sheets of clingfilm/plastic wrap and wrap them to make loose bags of beans.

Put the bags into the filo/Phyllo pastry cases and blind bake in the preheated oven for 10 minutes.

Remove from the oven and leave to cool. Take the bags of beans out, then re-glaze the inside of the filo/Phyllo basket with a little more beaten egg white. Return to the oven for a 2 minutes. Allow to cool for a couple of minutes, then carefully remove the pastry cases from the rings and transfer to a baking sheet.

Reduce the oven to 140°C (275°F) Gas 1.

Spoon the pumpkin mixture into the filo/Phyllo parcels, and bake in the cooled oven for 30–40 minutes, until the mixture is set.

Serve hot with a salad of rocket/arugula leaves and a drizzle of mustard oil over the top.

Courgette and Gruyère soufflé

PREPARE: **30 MINUTES** COOK: **15 MINUTES** SERVES: **4**

A cheese soufflé is a classic French recipe and is surprisingly easy to make. Here, the addition of courgette/zucchini adds a freshness and depth of flavour. I've added a little custard powder, too – a chef's trick to make the soufflé hold its shape and rise more evenly.

40 g/2½ tablespoons butter

30 g/2 tablespoons plain/all-purpose flour

250 ml/1 cup whole milk

1 teaspoon custard powder

1 teaspoon English mustard powder

100 g/¾ cup finely grated Gruyère cheese

50 g/⅔ cup grated courgette/zucchini

50 g/⅔ cup finely grated Parmesan cheese

4 eggs, separated

4 x 9-cm/3½-inch diameter ramekins, greased

Preheat the oven to 180°C (350°F) Gas 4.

First, make a roux. Put the butter and flour in a dry saucepan and set over a medium heat until the mixture forms small balls. Slowly, add the milk and whisk to combine into a smooth paste. Bring to a low simmer and add the custard powder, mustard powder, grated Gruyère and courgette/zucchini. Whisk to combine until the cheese has melted, then take off the heat and set aside to cool.

Next, prepare a bain marie. Half-fill a casserole dish with boiling water and set in the preheated oven.

Prepare the ramekins by sprinkling with Parmesan – it should stick to the butter used for greasing – before placing in the fridge to cool for at least 5 minutes.

Put the egg yolks in a large bowl and beat together with the roux until they form a glossy mixture. Whisk the egg whites separately until they form soft peaks, then, using a wooden spoon, fold into the soufflé mixture, a little at a time to make a light, airy batter.

Spoon the batter into the ramekins and use the back of a knife to form a level top. Run the tip of your thumb around the rim to leave an air gap between the soufflé top and the rim of the ramekin. This will help the soufflé to rise.

Carefully place the ramekins in the bain marie and cook for 12–14 minutes until they have risen and are golden on the top.

Remove from the oven and serve immediately.

Croquettes

PREPARE: **10 MINUTES** COOK: **5 MINUTES** SERVES: **4**

The perfect Monday night dinner; this dish uses up all the weekend's leftover mashed potatoes.

300 g/1½ cups leftover mashed potatoes or 450 g/1 lb. potatoes, peeled and roughly chopped

a good knob/pat of butter (optional), for preparing the mashed potatoes

100 ml/⅓ cup double/heavy cream (optional), for preparing the mashed potatoes

2 eggs

100 g/1 cup grated mixed cheese

2 slices bread, blitzed into breadcrumbs

vegetable oil, for frying

table salt, to season

Beetroot or Mushroom Ketchup (page 161), to serve

leftover vegetables or mixed salad leaves, to serve

If you don't have any leftover mashed potatoes, put the uncooked potatoes in a large saucepan, cover with boiling water and cook over a medium heat for 20–25 minutes until soft. Drain and mash with a little butter and cream.

Crack the eggs into a large mixing bowl and quickly whisk. Put the mashed potatoes into another bowl and add two-thirds of the whisked eggs, mix together.

Take a small handful of the mixture and flatten it to the size and shape of the palm of your hand. Holding it in your hand, pick a tablespoon-sized portion of the cheese and put it in the middle, before closing your hand and capturing the cheese inside. Roll it between your hands to form a short, fat, cigar-shaped croquette. Repeat with the rest of the mixture – you should have enough for eight.

Put the croquettes on a plate and leave to cool in the fridge for 30 minutes.

Preheat a deep-fryer or saucepan filled with vegetable oil to 180°C (350°F) on a temperature probe.

With the remaining egg in one bowl and the breadcrumbs seasoned with a good couple of pinches of table salt in another, firstly, place the croquettes into the egg, then the breadcrumbs, then into the hot oil. Cook for 4–5 minutes until golden. Carefully remove using a metal slotted spoon or tongs and drain on paper towels to dry off any excess oil.

Serve with beetroot or mushroom ketchup and a quick stir-fry of any leftover vegetables or salad leaves.

Potato Dauphinoise

PREPARE: **20 MINUTES** COOK: **1½ HOURS** SERVES: **4**

Dauphinoise is the king of all potato dishes. Perfectly cooked, it is soft and unctuous, has a crisp roasted top and creamy garlic running all the way through it.

150 ml/⅔ cup double/heavy cream

100 ml/⅓ cup whole milk

2 garlic cloves, crushed

600 g/1¼ lbs. Maris Piper or other floury potatoes, peeled and thinly sliced

table salt and ground white pepper, to season

Preheat the oven to 180°C (350°F) Gas 4.

Put the cream, milk and crushed garlic in a saucepan and set over a medium heat. Bring to a low simmer for 5 minutes.

Meanwhile, arrange the potato slices in layers in a loaf pan, slightly overlapping each slice. Between every couple of layers, sprinkle a good pinch of table salt and one of pepper (add more seasoning than you think you should). Continue until all of the potatoes are in the pan.

Slowly pour over the garlicky cream and milk mixture until it just covers the potatoes – add a little more cream and milk if necessary.

Cover with a loose foil lid to stop the top burning.

Transfer to the preheated oven and cook for 1½–2 hours. After 1 hour of cooking, check that the potatoes are softening by probing them with a sharp knife and press down on the top layer with a fish slice. Once the potatoes have softened, remove the foil, press the top layer down again with a fish slice and continue to bake for a final 20–30 minutes until it is golden on top.

Serve straight away or, even better, cover the top with foil and press with weights (a couple of cans of vegetables should do) to form a tightly packed loaf of Dauphinoise. Chill, then slice into portions and pan fry them in a little butter, before serving on a bed of warm salad leaves with a sprinkle of cheese on top.

Potato bowls with mushroom, garlic, spinach and ricotta

PREPARE: **10 MINUTES** COOK: **1 HOUR 15 MINUTES** SERVES: **4**

I love a jacket potato and these are the best! The second cooking of the potato skins makes them extra crunchy, which offers a delicious contrast to the fluffy, whipped potato and ricotta filling.

4 large Maris Piper or other floury potatoes

a good knob/pat of butter

250 g/½ lb. button mushrooms, quartered

100 g/1 cup spinach, washed

2 garlic cloves, crushed

a splash of balsamic vinegar

200 g/7 oz. ricotta cheese

table salt, to season

Preheat the oven to 180°C (350°F) Gas 4.

Clean, then prick the potatoes all over with a fork, before putting them in a microwave to cook for 20 minutes on high. Remove the potatoes from the microwave and cook in the preheated oven for 45 minutes.

While the potatoes are baking, Put a generous dollop of butter in a large, heavy-based frying pan/skillet and add a pinch of table salt. Heat the frying pan/skillet over a medium–high heat until the butter is sizzling, then add the chopped mushrooms and cook until golden. Do not stir the mushrooms while they are cooking or they will go soggy. Turn them once when they are golden, then add the spinach, garlic and balsamic vinegar, and take off the heat. Stir together – the residual heat from the pan will cook the garlic and spinach.

Remove the potatoes and carefully, using a dry kitchen cloth or oven gloves to hold them, cut the tops off, about one-third of the way from the top. Scoop out the cooked insides of the potatoes and reserve them. Keep the oven on.

Mix the cooked mushrooms, garlic and spinach with half of the scooped-out potato flesh and half of the ricotta cheese. Fold together, before refilling the potatoes with the mixture. Cover with the remaining ricotta, crumbled over the top and bake in the still-warm oven for 10 minutes. Serve hot.

Sweet potato chips

PREPARE: **5 MINUTES** COOK: **40 MINUTES** SERVES: **2-4**

Sweet potato chips are the perfect side dish to many meals, including the Fennel and Roast Tomato Lasagne on page 80.

100 ml/⅓ cup olive oil, plus extra to drizzle

1 teaspoon miso paste or ½ teaspoon Marmite yeast extract

750 g/1¾ lbs. sweet potatoes, peeled and cut into wedges

table salt and freshly ground black pepper, to season

Preheat the oven to 180°C (350°F) Gas 4.

Pour the olive oil into a large mixing bowl and add the miso paste or Marmite yeast extract. Toss the sweet potato wedges in the mixture until they are coated with oil and miso.

Spread the wedges out onto a baking sheet. Put in the preheated oven and cook for 40 minutes.

Remove from the oven, sprinkle with table salt and black pepper, and serve.

Pizza bianco

PREPARE: **15 MINUTES (PLUS 2 HOURS TO PROVE)** COOK: **25 MINUTES** SERVES: **4**

Pizzas are fun to make at home and so very easy. The pizza base recipe can be kept in the fridge for a few days, or frozen after you have baked it.

180 ml/^{3}/$_4$ cup warm water

5 g/1^3/$_4$ teaspoons fast-action dried yeast

300 g/2^1/$_4$ cups strong bread flour

a pinch of table salt

extra virgin olive oil, to drizzle

sea salt, to season

PIZZA TOPPING

200 g/1^3/$_4$ cups grated mozzarella cheese

200 g/2 cups grated Cheddar cheese

50 g/^{2}/$_3$ cup grated Parmesan cheese

1 onion, thinly sliced

a small bunch of fresh rosemary

250 g/9 oz. Maris Piper or other floury potatoes, peeled and very thinly sliced

4 baking sheets, oiled

Mix together the warm water, yeast, flour, salt and oil in a large mixing bowl using the tips of your fingers. Bring together in one ball.

Turn out onto an oiled surface and using the base of your hand stretch and work the dough for 10 minutes.

When the dough is smooth and a consistent texture, it is ready to prove. Drizzle a little olive oil into the base of the mixing bowl, oil the ball of dough and put it in the bowl. Cover with a clean kitchen cloth and put the bowl somewhere warm for 1^1/$_2$ hours (an airing cupboard or proving drawer is ideal for this).

Preheat the oven to 220°C (425°F) Gas 7.

After proving, the dough should be at least 2 times its original size. Gently turn it out onto an oiled surface and work the dough as before, to knock out the air.

Cut into four pieces and put onto separate oiled baking sheets. Stretch the dough with your fingertips until they are about 5 mm/^{1}/$_4$ inch thick. Don't worry about thinner or thicker areas as these add to the flavour and texture of the finished pizza.

Bake in batches in the preheated oven for 6 minutes. Turn the bases off the baking sheets and return to the oven directly on the shelf for another 3 minutes to crisp the base. Keep the oven on.

Sprinkle the cheeses evenly over the pizza bases with the onion slices and rosemary leaves.

Rinse the sliced potatoes and shake dry, then drizzle with olive oil to coat and arrange on top of the pizzas.

Return the pizzas to the still-warm oven for 10 minutes.

Check that the potato has turned golden before removing the pizzas. Drizzle with a little more oil and sprinkle with sea salt before serving.

Sweetcorn fritters

PREPARE: **5 MINUTES** COOK: **5 MINUTES** SERVES: **4**

Every New Zealand kid grows up with sweetcorn fritters as a regular treat. This is a very quick recipe but the fritters can also be cooked in advance and reheated in the oven when needed.

400 g/3 cups drained canned sweetcorn

30 g/2 tablespoons self-raising/rising flour

1 teaspoon baking powder

50 ml/3¹/₂ tablespoons double/heavy cream

a pinch of tables salt (optional)

butter, for frying

Sweet Chilli Sauce (page 159) and mixed salad leaves, to serve

Make the batter by mixing together the sweetcorn, flour, baking powder and cream in a large mixing bowl. If the sweetcorn was not kept in salted water, then add a pinch of table salt, too.

Set a heavy-based frying pan/skillet over a medium heat and add enough butter to cover the base when melted. When the butter starts to foam, place tablespoon-sized portions of the batter into the pan. Cook until the bases start to turn golden, then flip over and cook on the other side.

Serve hot or cold on a bed of mixed salad leaves with a dip of sweet chilli sauce. Alternatively, store in an airtight container and store in the freezer. To reheat, simply preheat the oven to 180°C (350°F) Gas 4, lay the fritters on a baking sheet and bake for 10 minutes to defrost and warm up.

Sweetcorn and soy

PREPARE: **1 MINUTE** COOK: **40 MINUTES** SERVES: **4**

Some recipes are just too simple and this is one of them. It's inspired by MasterChef UK 2011 winner, Tim Anderson; I had some wonderful soy and corn at his Namban Japanese restaurant. I was so inspired by the robust taste of it, I had to make some of my own.

4 cobs/ears of sweetcorn

100 g/7 tablespoons butter

2 tablespoons light soy sauce

Preheat the oven to 180°C (350°F) Gas 4.

Put the sweetcorn (in their husks) in a baking dish and bake in the preheated oven for 30 minutes. Remove from the oven and rest for 5 minutes. Carefully peel the husks off and set aside.

Heat the butter in a large frying pan/skillet set over a medium heat until it has melted and stops bubbling; you should be able to smell a nutty aroma as the butter starts to caramelize. The French term for this is *beurre noisette*, or hazelnut butter.

Quickly add the cobs/ears of corn and soy sauce. Immediately remove the pan from the heat and carefully roll the corn about in the butter.

Serve straight away with plenty of paper towels for messy fingers and faces!

Tip: Act quickly with a *beurre noisette* to take it off the heat, or it will burn.

Peas, beans and pulses

BROAD/FAVA BEANS • FRENCH BEANS • PEAS • LENTILS
BEANS • BEANSPROUTS

At some point in your life you must try a fresh pea, picked straight from the plant and popped from its pod. It's the essence of all things summery, fresh, sweet and delicious. After 5 minutes the flavour will have diminished, only a little, but enough to notice. Next spring, try growing a pea plant at home, you won't regret it!

Usually, I use frozen peas in cooking because they hold more of their flavour than 'fresh' peas. The freezing takes place very soon after they are picked so the sweetness is also frozen at that point, so unless you are picking and eating from your own garden, they just won't taste as good. The same is true for most beans and pulses, too, making frozen (or canned) usually best for cooking with. The peas in my Pea Panna Cottas on page 104 and Ricotta Tarts on page 107 are frozen but the dishes make the most of their lovely freshness of flavour to make light and tasty dishes.

Try making your own Homemade Baked Beans or a Smokey Cassoulet following the recipes on page 112. Both use a tomato and garlic base to create a filling and satisfying dish. Beans can also be light and tasty though, so try them in the Broad Bean Hummous on page 108 or add beansprouts in the Thai Salad on page 115.

Pea panna cottas with tomato salad

PREPARE: **10 MINUTES** COOK: **15 MINUTES (PLUS SETTING TIME)** SERVES: **4**

A savoury dessert or a sweet appetizer? – the choice is yours; peas are naturally sweet to taste and this dish is a fun way to make the most of their wonderful flavour.

100 ml/$\frac{1}{3}$ cup double/heavy cream

100 g/7 tablespoons butter

200 ml/$\frac{3}{4}$ cup vegetable stock

6 g/1$\frac{3}{4}$ teaspoons agar agar powder (setting agent)

300 g/2 cups frozen peas

10 cherry tomatoes, quartered

table salt, to season

white sugar, to season

balsamic vinegar, to drizzle

TO SERVE

a small bag of fresh pea shoots or rocket/arugula leaves

petals of 1 marigold flower

Put the cream, butter, stock and agar agar powder into a saucepan and set over a medium heat. Bring to a low simmer, then remove from the heat. Add the frozen peas and allow them to heat through for a couple of minutes. Blend using a handheld electric blender to a bright green pouring consistency.

Add a pinch of salt and 1 teaspoon of sugar and taste the mixture. Add a little more seasoning if needed.

Strain the mixture through a fine mesh sieve/strainer into a jug/pitcher and pour into moulds. Put in the fridge to set overnight.

Put the tomatoes in a bowl with a sprinkling of salt, sugar and balsamic vinegar. Toss to combine and set aside.

To serve, turn out the panna cottas by dipping the base of the moulds in hot, not boiling, water. When the panna cotta has released from the sides of the mould, turn the mould upside down and release onto serving plates. Spoon the tomato salad around the panna cottas and decorate with pea shoots or rocket/arugula and marigold petals.

Ricotta tarts with pea and mint

PREPARE: **30 MINUTES** COOK: **20 MINUTES** SERVES: **4**

These fresh and tasty tarts not only look beautiful, but give you the opportunity to make your own cheese, which is simple and fun to do.

250 g/9 oz. puff pastry

200 g/7 oz. ricotta or curd cheese (see below)

100 g/¾ cup frozen peas

a bunch of fresh mint

1 egg, beaten

sea salt and freshly ground black pepper, to season

CURD CHEESE

1.5 litres/quarts whole milk

2 teaspoons table salt

2 tablespoons white wine vinegar

a 15-cm/6-inch diameter baking ring

Preheat the oven to 180°C (350°F) Gas 4.

Roll out the puff pastry on a lightly floured surface to a thickness of about 3 mm/⅛ inch.

Using the baking ring as a guide and a small, sharp knife, cut eight pastry circles. Do not press the circles out using the ring, or the edges will be pinched together and the pastry will not rise.

On four of the circles, cut a second circle out of the middle, about 10 cm/4 inches in diameter. This will leave you with four rings of puff pastry.

Now you need to stick the rings onto the remaining circles, which will form the tarts. Lightly moisten one side of the rings with a little water and place them on top of the circles. Gently, transfer to a baking sheet.

Brush the rings with a little beaten egg and, using a fork, poke small holes in the centre circle of each tart. Sprinkle with a little sea salt and bake in the preheated oven for 10 minutes, until the tops are risen and have turned golden. Remove from the oven and allow to cool. Reduce the heat to 140°C (275°F) Gas 1.

In a large mixing bowl, gently mash the ricotta or curd cheese, peas and a few leaves of chopped mint together. Spoon the mixture into the tart cases. Overfill the cases, so the mixture is spilling over the top. Return to the cooled oven for 20 minutes.

Remove, sprinkle with black pepper, decorate with a couple of mint leaves and serve immediately.

How to make curd cheese: Pour the milk into a saucepan. Add the table salt and set over a medium heat. Bring the milk to about 70°C (190°F) when tested using a temperature probe. Add the white wine vinegar and stir gently. The milk should start to curdle. Leave the milk for a couple of minutes to separate into curds and whey.

Line a fine mesh sieve/strainer with a fine cloth, muslin/cheesecloth or clean kitchen cloth and set over a large mixing bowl. Strain the mixture through this – you should be left with about 250 g/9 oz. of curds in the sieve/strainer.

Set in a fridge, leaving the curds in the sieve/strainer over the bowl, to completely drain for about 1 hour. Remove from the fridge and twist your cloth around the strained curds to press them together, forming a simple cheese, which is ready to use.

Broad bean hummous

PREPARE: **20 MINUTES** COOK: **5 MINUTES** SERVES: **4**

This is a fresh alternative to traditional hummous. The nutty flavour of broad/fava beans works really well with lemon and the sesame of the tahini.

300 g/2¼ cups fresh broad/fava beans

400 g/1½ cups canned chickpeas/garbanzo beans, drained

50 g/¼ cup tahini

2 roasted garlic cloves (see Note)

grated zest and freshly squeezed juice of 1 lemon

table salt and freshly ground black pepper, to season

toasted bread, to serve

Put the broad/fava beans in a saucepan of cold, unsalted water and set over a medium heat. Bring to a low simmer and continue to simmer for 5 minutes. Drain, then put in a bowl of cold water and chill in the fridge to halt the cooking. After a few minutes, remove the outer skins and discard, reserving the inner beans to use in the hummous.

Put the beans and the remaining ingredients in a large mixing bowl with ½ teaspoon of salt. Blend to a fine paste using a handheld electric blender. Taste the mixture and add extra salt if needed.

Sprinkle with black pepper and serve right away with toasted bread or cover and store in the fridge for up to 4 days.

Note: To roast garlic, place a whole bulb of garlic on a baking sheet and cook in a preheated oven at 180°C (350°F) Gas 4 for 45 minutes. You can easily do this while you're cooking something else and save it in the fridge until you need it. You will now have a bulb of soft garlic paste that can be squeezed, like a tube of toothpaste, one clove at a time.

Pea and wasabi dip

PREPARE: **15 MINUTES** COOK: **2 MINUTES** SERVES: **4**

A quick recipe that makes use of the freezer and store-cupboard to whip up a fresh and spicy dip for afternoon snacking. I find the punchy flavour and heat of wasabi quite addictive!

½ small red onion, finely diced

white wine vinegar to cover

150 g/1¼ cup frozen peas, slightly defrosted

1 teaspoon wasabi powder

1 teaspoon light soy sauce

grated zest of 1 lemon

a pinch of table salt, to season

fresh vegetable sticks or cheese crackers, to serve

Put the onion in a small bowl and just cover with the vinegar. Set aside to infuse for 15 minutes.

Put the peas, wasabi, soy and lemon zest in a jug/pitcher of about 300-ml/10-oz. capacity that is only slightly larger in diameter than the blade end of a handheld electric blender. Purée the contents to make a smooth, thick paste. Taste and, if you like your dip hotter, add a little more wasabi, then blend again.

Add a heaped teaspoon of drained red onion pieces and a good pinch of table salt. Mix together with a spoon.

Serve as a dip with fresh vegetable sticks, or on crackers.

Huevos rancheros

PREPARE: **10 MINUTES** COOK: **40 MINUTES** SERVES: **4**

Homely, warming and fun food for a family gathering or for breakfast the morning after...

2 onions, finely chopped

1 jalapeño pepper, finely chopped

1 chipotle pepper, finely chopped

2 garlic cloves, finely chopped

a bunch of fresh coriander/cilantro, stalks finely chopped and leaves reserved

400 g/2 cups canned chopped tomatoes

400 g/2 cups canned kidney beans, drained and mashed

4 eggs

8 tortillas

vegetable oil, for frying

table salt, to season

Tabasco sauce, to taste

sour cream, to serve

Preheat the oven to 180°C (350°F) Gas 4.

Add a little vegetable oil to cover the bottom of a saucepan. Add the onions with a good sprinkle of table salt and set over a low heat until the onions are cooked through and glassy. Add the peppers, garlic and coriander stalks and leave on a low heat for another few minutes until the garlic and onions are just starting to brown.

Add the tomatoes and mashed kidney beans and heat until the mixture is simmering. Add a few generous glugs of Tabasco sauce, to taste.

Transfer the mixture to a large casserole dish and carefully crack the eggs on top, spaced around the dish.

Bake in the preheated oven for 15–20 minutes until the egg whites are just cooked. Warm the tortillas in the oven for the final few minutes of cooking.

Serve the casserole dish in the middle of your table, with the warm tortillas, some cold sour cream and a large spoon to serve with.

Mulligatawny soup

PREPARE: **10 MINUTES** COOK: **40 MINUTES** SERVES: **4**

The literal translation of mulligatawny is 'spicy water'. This version of Mulligatawny soup has Indian spice aromas and flavours but uses the barley and lentils to add texture.

2 teaspoons each of ground coriander, ground cumin and ground turmeric

1 teaspoon cayenne pepper

4 carrots, finely chopped

2 celery sticks, thinly sliced

2 onions, finely chopped

2 garlic cloves, crushed

200 g/1 cup red lentils

200 g/1 cup pearl barley

30 g/4 tablespoons thinly sliced ginger

a small bunch of fresh coriander/cilantro, finely chopped

1/2 lemon, to squeeze

vegetable oil, for frying

100 ml/1/3 cup double/heavy cream, to serve (optional)

Add a generous splash of vegetable oil to a large saucepan, set over a medium heat and when the oil begins to shimmer from the heat, add the ground coriander, cumin, turmeric and cayenne. Stir for about 30 seconds. Add the chopped carrots, celery and onions. Continue cooking until the onions are glassy and just starting to turn golden, then add the garlic and continue to cook for another 30 seconds, stirring continuously.

Add 2 litres/quarts of water and heat to a low simmer. Continue to simmer for 20 minutes, then use a handheld electric blender to purée the vegetables. Add the lentils and barley and leave to simmer for a further 20 minutes.

Before serving, add the coriander/cilantro with a good squeeze of lemon.

Tip: Add the double/heavy cream if you want a richer and less spicy soup.

Homemade baked beans

PREPARE: **15 MINUTES** COOK: **15 MINUTES** SERVES: **4**

Homemade baked beans have so much more flavour with less salt and sugar than the canned varieties you might be used to. This recipe is easy to make, fun for first time cooks, young or old.

1 teaspoon smoked paprika

1 teaspoon dried ground coriander

2 garlic cloves, crushed

40 g/2$\frac{1}{2}$ tablespoons concentrated tomato purée/paste

2 teaspoons black treacle/molasses

800 g/5$\frac{1}{3}$ cups canned cannellini beans or 500 g/2$\frac{1}{2}$ cups dried cannellini beans soaked overnight in cold water, drained

100 g/1 cup grated Cheddar cheese

Worcestershire or 'Shire' sauce (page 159)

vegetable oil, for frying

table salt, to season

toasted sourdough, to serve

Preheat the oven to 160°C (325°F) Gas 3.

Just cover the base of a frying pan/skillet with vegetable oil and set over a low heat. Add the paprika and coriander. When the spices start to sizzle, add the garlic and a pinch of table salt and leave until they're just starting to turn golden. Add the tomato purée/paste and black treacle/molasses and stir all together. Continue to cook for a couple of minutes, then add the beans. Finally, add enough water to just cover the beans.

Pour the mixture into a small baking dish, cover with the grated cheese and splash with Worcestershire or shire sauce and bake in the preheated oven for 15 minutes.

Remove from the oven and serve straight from the dish with toasted sourdough on the side.

Smokey cassoulet

PREPARE: **20 MINUTES** COOK: **20 MINUTES** SERVES: **4**

This European dish is wonderful comfort food that should be savoured.

500 ml/2 cups vegetable stock

1 red (bell) pepper

2 onions, finely diced

75 g/5 tablespoons butter

2 garlic cloves, crushed

140 g/$\frac{1}{2}$ cup concentrated tomato purée/paste

400 g/2$\frac{2}{3}$ cups canned cannellini beans

400 g/2$\frac{2}{3}$ cups canned Haricot/navy beans

smoked sweet paprika, to taste

chilli/hot red pepper flakes, to taste

table salt, to season

dried onions, to serve

Pour the stock into a saucepan and set over a medium heat. Bring to a simmer and continue to simmer for 10–15 minutes until it has reduced by two-thirds.

Preheat a grill pan over a high heat. Cook the red (bell) pepper on the very hot pan to just blacken the flesh, before dicing it into 5-mm/$\frac{1}{4}$-inch dice.

In a large, deep frying pan/skillet set over a low heat, cook the onions with the butter and a generous pinch of salt until the onions are starting to turn golden. Add the crushed garlic and continue to cook for a few more minutes. Add the tomato purée/paste, the stock and blackened red (bell) pepper and bring to a low simmer. Continue to simmer for 10 minutes, then add the beans and enough water to just cover them. Add 1 teaspoon of smoked paprika and a pinch of chilli/hot red pepper flakes to the mixture and continue to simmer for 5 minutes. Taste and add more paprika or chilli/hot red pepper flakes to taste. Finally add $\frac{1}{2}$ teaspoon of table salt and stir in. Ensure the mixture doesn't dry out by adding a little water as necessary.

The cassoulet, like all stews, will taste better if left in the fridge for a day or two and reheated but can be served immediately. Serve in bowls with a generous sprinkle of dried onions on top.

Thai salad

PREPARE: **20 MINUTES** SERVES: **4**

Hot, sweet and sour are the key flavours of a good dish from Thailand and are all present here.

a small bunch of fresh coriander/cilantro

a bunch of spring onions/scallions, finely chopped

1 stalk fresh lemon grass, finely chopped

2 red Bird's eye chillies/chiles, deseeded and finely chopped

2 shallots, finely chopped

50 g/2 oz. fresh galangal (or 30 g/1 oz. fresh ginger), peeled and grated

50 g/1 cup toasted coconut slices

grated zest of 1 lime

200 g/3½ cups beansprouts

75 g/⅔ cup roasted cashew nuts, roughly chopped

200 g/1½ cups cubed firm tofu

DRESSING

100 ml/⅓ cup vegetable oil

30 ml/2 tablespoons sesame oil

seeds of 2 red Bird's eye chillies/chiles

2 teaspoons palm sugar/jaggery

freshly squeezed juice of 1 lime

Make the salad dressing by putting all the dressing ingredients in a sealed bottle or jar and shaking vigorously until the sugar is dissolved. Set aside.

Finely chop the coriander/cilantro stalks, setting the leaves aside. Toss with the spring onions/scallions, lemon grass, chillies/chiles and shallots in a large mixing bowl.

Add the galangal or ginger, then add the lime zest and half of the cashews.

To serve, divide half of the beansprouts between four plates. Arrange the tofu on top. Mix the remaining beansprouts with the other salad ingredients and pile on top of the tofu. Dress generously with the salad dressing and finish with a sprinkle of coriander/cilantro leaves and the remaining cashew nuts.

Runner beans with aubergine pasta

PREPARE: **10 MINUTES** COOK: **10 MINUTES** SERVES: **4**

This dish is vibrant and colourful with surprising and tasty flavours. From nutty aubergine/eggplant pasta to peppery nasturtiums, this dish is fun to make and to eat.

1 large aubergine/eggplant, peeled and very thinly sliced into ribbons

2 red onions, finely diced

50 g/⅓ cup pine nuts

200 g/2 cups trimmed French or runner/green beans

grated zest and freshly squeezed juice of ½ lemon

vegetable oil, for frying

table salt, to season

100 g/¾ cup cubed feta cheese and nasturtium flowers and leaves, to serve

Pour enough oil to cover the bottom of a large, heavy-based saucepan, up to about 2 mm/¹⁄₁₆ inch deep. Set over a medium heat and when the pan is hot enough (it will sizzle when a piece of onion is dropped into it), add the aubergine/eggplant ribbons and turn them quickly while they cook to coat them with oil. Add the onions and pine nuts. Cook for a few minutes, turning frequently until the onions are starting to turn golden. Cover with a good couple of pinches of salt and turn again before adding the trimmed beans.

Cook the mixture for a further 2 minutes to heat the beans through, then squeeze lemon juice over the pan and add the zest. Serve with the feta crumbled over the top and decorated with nasturtium leaves and flowers.

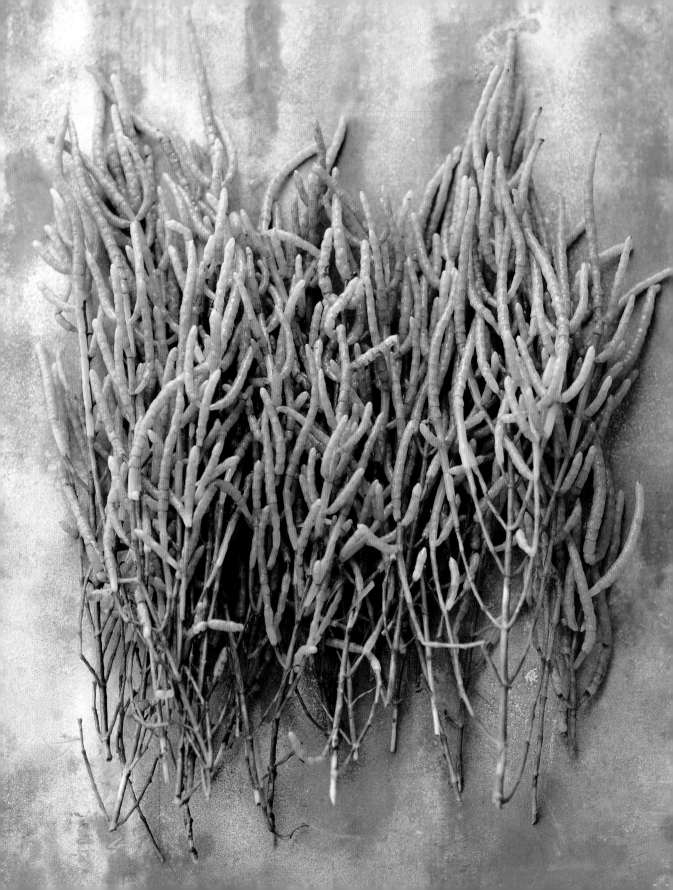

Stalks, stems and soft leaves

ASPARAGUS • LETTUCE • ROCKET/ARUGULA • WATERCRESS • ARTICHOKES • SAMPHIRE

My favourite months of the year happily coincide with the asparagus season. With spring comes this delightful plant and less is more when it comes to cooking asparagus, it only needs a few minutes of heat to cook. From a rich Asparagus Risotto (page 125) to a fresh, light Asparagus Tagliatelle and Pea Verrine (page 122) or just simply griddled with a Hollandaise sauce (page 121), asparagus is so versatile and simple to cook.

Neither of my artichoke recipes require any skills to peel and trim the choke. I unashamedly use jarred artichoke hearts in my frittata recipe on page 118 – all the hard work has been done for you and they taste delicious straight from the jar. If you can get fresh artichokes, then simply poach them in salted water and serve with cheese and garlic butter as on page 118 for a spectacularly simple dish that's fun, messy finger food at its best.

Samphire is now finding its way into supermarkets, usually near the fish counter. Try this unusual sea vegetable in a simple tart (page 126) with chilli/chile and strong feta cheese, which balances the saltiness of this delicious vegetable.

Salads are so often badly made, an afterthought. I've written a Caesar Salad (page 130) and Waldorf Salad Wraps (page 133) as my take on these classic meals, simple to make but classics for a reason... the flavours work so well. My Pimm's Salad (page 129) is fun and perfect for a hot summery day, as is the Rocket, Black Olive, Feta and Orange Salad (page 134). Both use fruit to add sweetness and to off-set the bitterness of salad leaves.

Artichoke frittata

PREPARE: **15 MINUTES** COOK: **15 MINUTES** SERVES: **4**

I have a love of jarred artichokes... the ones in glass jars on deli counters. They are delicious eaten straight from the jar or heated very gently but they taste their absolute best when paired with salty flavours, like the feta cheese in this frittata.

100 g/3¹/₂ oz. new potatoes
6 eggs
300 ml/1¹/₃ cups double/heavy cream
100 ml/¹/₃ cup whole milk
8 artichokes from a jar
150 g/5 oz. feta cheese
a generous pinch each of table salt and ground white pepper
freshly ground black pepper, to season

4 x 15-cm/6-inch diameter ovenproof dishes

Preheat the oven to 180°C (350°F) Gas 4.

Scrub the new potatoes and put them in a pan with enough water to cover them. Bring to the boil and cook for 10 minutes until tender. Drain, then dice or halve them into about 1-cm/³/₈-inch pieces.

In a mixing bowl, quickly whisk together the eggs, cream, milk and salt and white pepper.

Halve the artichokes and set aside. Roughly chop the feta until it forms a rough crumb.

Arrange the artichokes and potatoes in the ovenproof dishes. Pour over equal amounts of the egg mixture, sprinkle over the feta cheese crumb and give each a good crack of black pepper.

Cook in the preheated oven (in batches if your oven won't hold all four dishes) for 12–15 minutes, until cooked and starting to turn golden on top. Remove from the oven and rest for a couple of minutes before serving.

Artichoke with garlic butter

PREPARE: **5 MINUTES** COOK: **40 MINUTES** SERVES: **4**

Stunning to look at and simple to cook, an artichoke often scares cooks due to its rugged appearance and often complicated methods to cook and prepare. I like my artichoke simply cooked and served with garlic butter as finger food. Serve with plenty of napkins and a teaspoon to remove the choke.

4 globe artichokes
200 g/1³/₄ sticks salted butter
2 garlic cloves, crushed
50 g/²/₃ cup grated Parmesan cheese
freshly ground black pepper, to season

Trim the base of each artichoke so it can stand upright. Slice across the artichoke top, about 3 cm/1¹/₄ inch from the top, to display the inner leaf patterns.

Transfer the artichokes to a large covered pan of salted water and simmer over a low heat for 30 minutes.

Heat the butter in a small pan until it just begins to foam. Add the crushed garlic to the foaming butter and remove from the heat; stir a couple of times to distribute the garlic and set aside.

Place the steaming hot artichokes in four serving bowls. Drizzle with the garlic butter and top with Parmesan. Finish with a sprinkle of black pepper and serve.

To eat the artichoke, pluck each petal and squeeze the petal between your teeth pulling out the fleshy centre from the base. When all the petals have been eaten, remove the furry choke with a teaspoon then eat the core of the artichoke, mopping up the remaining butter and cheese. This is messy eating at its delicious best!

Asparagus with hollandaise sauce

PREPARE: **15 MINUTES** COOK: **5 MINUTES** SERVES: **4**

Asparagus and freshly made lemony hollandaise is a real treat. I prefer asparagus when it's griddled which gives it smokiness and bite; a much more grown-up dish than boiled asparagus.

250 g/2 sticks plus 1 tablespoon butter

4 egg yolks

grated zest and freshly squeezed juice of 1 lemon

20 asparagus spears

vegetable oil, to coat

table salt and ground white pepper, to season

To make the hollandaise sauce, melt the butter in a saucepan set over a medium heat. Allow it to bubble for a few minutes to cook off the water. Set aside until it is just cool enough to touch.

You will need a handheld electric blender and a jug/pitcher of about 300-ml/10-oz. capacity that is only slightly larger in diameter than the blade end of the blender for following this method.

Put the egg yolks, lemon juice and a pinch of salt and pepper into the jug/pitcher. Slowly place the stick blender into the jug/pitcher, capturing the yolks under the blade. While continuously blending pour the melted butter in, taking about 30 seconds, then slowly pull the blender out to combine the butter and yolks. This will form a sauce; it really is that simple.

Next, prepare the asparagus spears. Snap them by bending from the base and discard the woody end, trim the stalk and take off the horns to leave a smooth asparagus spear. Lightly oil and season the asparagus with a little table salt.

Preheat a grill pan over a medium–high heat. Carefully place the asparagus spears in the pan and cook until they are just starting to blacken, turn over and repeat.

Serve simply on a warm plate with a generous dollop of hollandaise sauce, topped with a sprinkle of lemon zest and ground white pepper.

Asparagus tagliatelle and pea verrine

PREPARE: **15 MINUTES** COOK: **10 MINUTES** SERVES: **4**

Asparagus are best enjoyed in season. Don't bother with imported ones as they will lack freshness and flavour. Verrines are small, cold dishes served in glasses rather than on plates.

16 asparagus spears

100 g/³/₄ cup frozen peas

100 g/¹/₂ cup cream cheese

2 teaspoons double/heavy cream

grated zest and freshly squeezed juice of 1 lemon

a handful of pea shoots or wild rocket/arugula

first-press rapeseed oil, to drizzle

freshly ground black pepper, to season

Snap the asparagus by bending from the base and discard the woody end, trim the stalk and take off the horns to leave a smooth asparagus spear. Using a peeler or a fine mandoline, carefully make thin strips the length of the spear; you should get 5–6 strips per spear to make asparagus 'tagliatelle'.

Cook the asparagus strips and peas in a pan of boiling salted water for 3 minutes, then immediately plunge them in a large bowl of ice-cold water to stop them cooking any further.

After a couple of minutes, remove from the cold water and pat dry with paper towels. Drizzle with rapeseed oil and sprinkle lightly with black pepper and set aside.

Put the cream cheese, cream and lemon juice in a large mixing bowl and whisk together to make a mousse.

To serve, divide the peas between four glasses, then cover with a layer of the cream cheese mouse. Form the asparagus tagliatelle into loose balls and put into the glasses. Top with pea shoots or wild rocket/arugula and lemon zest to finish.

Asparagus risotto

PREPARE: **15 MINUTES** COOK: **15 MINUTES (PLUS 45 MINUTES TO MAKE THE STOCK)** SERVES: **4**

This is a great way to enjoy the flavour of asparagus and the dramatic appearance of a vibrant green risotto makes it great fun, too.

4 carrots, peeled

2 celery sticks

3 brown onions

400 g/14 oz. asparagus

80 g/1¼ cups spinach leaves, washed

2 garlic cloves, finely sliced

350 g/2 cups arborio rice

200 ml/¾ cup white wine

80 g/1¼ cup Parmesan cheese

grated zest of ½ lemon

a knob/pat of butter

olive oil, for frying

table salt, to season

Firstly, make an asparagus stock. Finely dice the carrots, celery and 2 of the brown onions and put in a pan with 1 litre/1¾ pints of water.

Trim about 2.5 cm/1 inch from the base of the asparagus spears and discard. Trim a further 2.5 cm/1 inch from the base of the spears, finely slice them and place in the stock water. Bring the stock to a low simmer and cook for 45 minutes. Add the spinach and simmer for 2 minutes, then blend the stock with a handheld electric blender until smooth.

Add a little oil to a large heavy-based non-stick pan. Finely dice the remaining onion and add to the pan with the garlic and cook over a very low heat until just translucent. Add the rice and cook, gently stirring, until the rice is covered with oil and starts to go opaque. Add the wine and simmer until the wine is nearly all absorbed. Stirring constantly, add half of the asparagus stock and a pinch of salt and continue cooking on a low simmer until all of the stock is absorbed. Continue adding the remaining stock a little at a time until the rice is cooked and has just a little bite when tasted (there should be no excess liquid).

To finish, stir in the Parmesan cheese, lemon zest, asparagus tips and a knob/pat of butter. Serve immediately.

Samphire tart with brown butter dressing

PREPARE: **15 MINUTES** COOK: **15 MINUTES** SERVES: **4**

Samphire can now be found in the fish section of many supermarkets and its sweet, salty taste balances well with chillies/chiles, shallots and nutty butter. If you can't find samphire, this recipe will work well with asparagus but you'll need to add a good sprinkle of sea salt.

6 shallots, thinly sliced

100 g/7 tablespoons butter

200 g/7 oz. ready-rolled puff pastry

150 g/5$\frac{1}{2}$ oz. samphire

4 red chillies/chiles, thinly sliced

100 g/$\frac{3}{4}$ cup cubed feta cheese

Preheat the oven to 200°C (400°F) Gas 5.

Put the shallots in a saucepan with the butter and set over a medium heat. Heat until the butter is foaming. Leave on the heat until the foaming starts to reduce, then remove immediately and allow to cool. You should get a distinctive nutty aroma from the cooked butter.

Unroll the puff pastry onto a floured baking sheet and trim with a sharp knife to 30 x 20 cm/12 x 8 inches. Bake in the preheated oven for 10 minutes until the pastry is just starting to turn golden and has risen. Allow to cool for a few minutes, then using a sharp knife, cut a line halfway through the pastry about 2 cm/$\frac{3}{4}$ inch from the sides. Press the inner pastry down using a fish slice to flatten slightly.

Check the samphire shoots for any woody bases and remove them. Tear the samphire into 2-cm/$\frac{3}{4}$-inch pieces and set aside.

Scoop the shallots out of the butter in the saucepan. Scatter around the inner pastry section along with some of the butter. Scatter the samphire and, chillies/chiles (use as many or as few as you like) around the tart and crumble over the feta.

Return the tart to the oven for 5 minutes, until the feta starts to melt and the pastry turns golden brown and crispy.

Remove from the oven, drizzle a little more brown butter over the tart and serve immediately.

Pimm's salad

PREPARE: **10 MINUTES** SERVES: **4**

Pimm's No. 1 Cup is traditionally served with mint, cucumber and a medley of chopped fresh summer fruits. This is my take, using the cocktail garnishes as a base for a quick and fun summery salad, perfect for al fresco lunches.

150 g/1^1/$_2$ cups strawberries, hulled and thinly sliced

1 large cucumber, peeled

a small bunch of fresh mint

grated zest and freshly squeezed juice of 1 lemon

50 g/1 cup fresh rocket/arugula

50 g/1 cup fresh watercress

150 ml/^{2}/$_3$ cup olive oil

20 ml/1^1/$_2$ tablespoons white wine vinegar

50 ml/3^1/$_2$ tablespoons Pimm's No. 1 cup or other summer gin cup

1 lemon, sliced into four wedges

Put the strawberries in a large mixing bowl and set aside.

Using a peeler, make long ribbons of the cucumber and add to the bowl with the strawberries. Discard the centre of the cucumber.

Pick two-thirds of the mint leaves and crush them a little before adding to the bowl; save the remaining leaves to dress the salad.

Add the lemon zest, rocket/arugula and watercress; checking they are cleaned and any large stalks are removed. Toss the leaves together to combine and coat in flavour.

Make a vinaigrette by pouring the lemon juice, olive oil, white wine vinegar and Pimm's into a jar with a screw-top lid. Tighten the lid and shake well to combine.

Pour about one-quarter of the vinaigrette down the side of the bowl with the salad ingredients and turn the salad over several times to coat.

To serve, arrange the salad on four plates and dress with the remaining mint leaves and a wedge of lemon. Pour the remaining vinaigrette into a jug/pitcher and bring to the table with a serving spoon.

Caesar salad

PREPARE: **20 MINUTES** SERVES: **4**

This salad was invented during the prohibition era by chef Caesar Cardini (of Italian descent) in Tijuana, Mexico, for American tourists. A lot of recipes for a Caesar salad add anchovies to the dressing; to me, this detracts from the clean flavours of garlic and fresh, charred lettuce that work so well together.

200 ml/³/₄ cup extra virgin olive oil, plus extra to drizzle

2 garlic cloves, crushed

4 slices sourdough bread, cut into 1-cm/³/₈-inch cubes

2 Cos/romaine lettuce heads, halved lengthways

freshly squeezed juice of ¹/₂ lemon

1 egg yolk

100 g/3¹/₂ oz. Parmesan cheese

Worcestershire or 'Shire' Sauce (page 159)

Firstly, you need to make garlic oil. Heat the oil and crushed garlic cloves in a pan to over 85°C (217°F), then leave to cool for at least an hour, while the flavours infuse.

Preheat the oven to 180°C (350°F) Gas 4.

Toss the sourdough cubes in the garlic oil until evenly coated. Spread out on a baking sheet and cook in the preheated oven for 20 minutes or until golden. Once removed from the oven, they will continue to crisp up even more as they cool.

Drizzle a little of the oil over the cut surface of the lettuce heads. Preheat a grill pan over a high heat and place the lettuce cut-side down in the pan. Cook for a few minutes until just starting to blacken.

Make a salad dressing by putting the garlic oil, the lemon juice and egg yolk in a jar with a screw-top lid, tightening the lid and shaking to combine.

To serve, arrange the lettuce halves, cut-side up, on plates. Finely grate half of the Parmesan over the top – it should begin to melt. Sprinkle the croutons over the plate.

Dress the salad generously with the salad dressing, then drizzle with a little Worcestershire or 'Shire' sauce and shave the remaining Parmesan over the top before serving.

Waldorf salad wraps

PREPARE: **10 MINUTES** SERVES: **4**

These Waldorf-style salad wraps can be served as fun canapés or as a light meal. They are both tasty and fun to eat.

2 little Gem/Bibb lettuce heads

grated zest and freshly squeezed juice of 1 lemon

2 green apples, cored and diced

100 ml/$\frac{1}{3}$ cup No-egg Mayonnaise (page 158)

6 celery sticks, sliced

150 g/1$\frac{1}{2}$ cups walnut halves

90 g/generous 1 cup pea shoots

60 g/generous 1 cup fresh wild rocket/arugula

Take off a couple of the outer leaves of the lettuces and discard. Choose 12 good leaves and set them aside. Finely chop the remaining lettuce and put in a large mixing bowl.

In a separate bowl, squeeze some lemon juice over the apple pieces and toss to coat. Add the dairy-free mayonnaise, lemon zest, celery, apple and the walnut halves. Toss together to generously coat all the ingredients.

Reserve some of the pea shoots for dressing the dish then mix together the remaining pea shoots, chopped lettuce, rocket/arugula and a squeeze of lemon juice.

To serve, place 3 reserved lettuce leaves on each plate; put the mixed salad on top, then the celery, apple and walnut mayonnaise on top of that. Dress with a few pea shoots and serve.

Rocket, black olive, feta and orange salad

PREPARE: **10 MINUTES** SERVES: **4**

Hot rocket/arugula leaves bring this Mediterranean-style salad alive, making it perfect for summer dining. Always buy the best extra virgin olive oil and olives you can find.

100 g/³⁄₄ cup cubed feta cheese

2 oranges

2 stalks fresh thyme

60 g/generous 1 cup fresh rocket/arugula

1 red onion, thinly sliced into rings

toasted flaked/slivered almonds

100 g/1 cup pitted black olives

extra virgin olive oil, to drizzle

sea salt, to season

Crumble the feta cheese into a large mixing bowl.

Zest the oranges and set aside. Cut the peel and pith from the oranges, then slice the segments out by using a small, sharp knife between the membranes and add to the bowl.

Pick the thyme leaves from the stalks and add to the bowl.

Add the remaining ingredients and toss to fully combine.

Drizzle with ample olive oil and sprinkle with a good pinch of sea salt before serving.

Fungi

MUSHROOMS · TRUFFLES

So often when asked for a vegetarian option, the request is closely followed by a rather plaintive 'not a mushroom risotto please!'. Now, don't get me wrong, I love mushroom risotto. I make a dried stock using dehydrated powder of mushrooms I've collected during the season (especially puffballs) simply dried and blitzed in a food processor. A glass of white wine, a little cheese and butter and a couple of tablespoons of mushroom powder and you have an amazing(!) risotto.

The recipes in this section demonstrate exactly what I say in the introduction to the book – treat good vegetables in the same way you would treat any other produce. I know mushrooms aren't strictly vegetables but they form a cornerstone of many vegetarian diets.

Go easy when using truffles, they can easily overpower a dish. If using an oil or infusion, then use the best you can get and use it sparingly. Truffle flavour comes mostly from aroma, not from taste, so whether thinly sliced or freshly grated truffle creates far more flavour than thickly sliced truffle, and is a lot more cost effective, too.

The combination of Portobello mushroom and smoked potato in The Best Burger on page 145 makes for the tastiest burger I've ever eaten; it takes a little work but you will be delighted with the results. The light and airy Champagne Mushrooms on page 138 are a total contrast, they are so light and tasty, a wonderful first course or light lunch. A Puffball Steak with Chips and Béarnaise Sauce on page 149 is nothing like the wimpy 'veggie' dishes many meat-eaters associate with vegetarian diets – it's so delicious as a meal that you'll cook it again and again. So don't be afraid to use these delicious forest delights. I know I'm not.

Champagne mushrooms

PREPARE: **20 MINUTES** COOK: **20 MINUTES** SERVES: **4**

Mushrooms have a rich flavour when roasted. Add Jerusalem artichoke, a hint of garlic and the lightness of sparkling wine and you have a stunning dinner party first course. Try the recipe with parsnips if Jerusalem artichokes are out of season.

200 g/7 oz. Jerusalem artichokes, peeled and thinly sliced

1 small shallot, finely diced

1 garlic clove, thinly sliced

200 ml/³/4 cup Champagne or Prosecco

4 large Portobello mushrooms, stems removed

50 ml/3¹/2 tablespoons vegetable oil

50 g/²/3 cup Parmesan cheese

50 g/²/3 cup flaked/slivered almonds

butter, for frying

Preheat a large frying pan/skillet over a low heat and add enough butter to just cover the base when melted. When the butter begins to sizzle, add the artichoke slices, shallot and garlic and cook for 5 minutes on low until they start to brown.

Add the Champagne and continue to heat for a couple of minutes until the volume of liquid has reduced by half. This will act as the filling. Set aside.

Preheat the oven to 180°C (350°F) Gas 4.

Brush the outside of the mushrooms with the vegetable oil to coat, then arrange the mushrooms on a baking sheet. Use some scrunched up foil to hold the mushrooms in place if necessary. Fill the mushrooms with the filling and sprinkle the Parmesan and flaked/slivered almonds over the top.

Bake in the preheated oven for 15–20 minutes until the almonds are browned and the Parmesan has melted.

Remove from the oven and serve immediately with a glass of Champagne.

Mushroom parfait

PREPARE: **20 MINUTES** COOK: **30 MINUTES** SERVES: **4**

This is a wonderful mushroom pâté, inspired by one given to me by the talented chef Stosie from The Parkers Arms pub in northern England. It makes a great canapé or small appetizer.

25 ml/1½ tablespoons Pernod

grated zest and freshly squeezed juice of 1 lemon

50 g/2 oz. dried wild mushrooms

400 ml/1²/₃ cups double/heavy cream

400 g/14 oz. fresh field or button mushrooms, thinly sliced

butter, for frying

vegetable oil, for frying

table salt, to season

To serve

Vegetable Pickles (page 166)

Mushroom Ketchup (page 161)

toasted seeded bread

1 endive or chicory/Belgian endive head

2 jalapeño peppers

a terrine dish or loaf pan, lined with clingfilm/plastic wrap

In a small saucepan, heat the Pernod and lemon juice over a medium heat until just simmering. Add the dried wild mushrooms and a little cream, if needed to cover them, and bring it back to simmer. Take it off the heat and leave for 20 minutes until the mushrooms are hydrated and soft.

Add a little butter and vegetable oil to a frying pan/skillet. Add the sliced field or button mushrooms and pan-fry until just browned. Make sure the pan is sizzling hot before you put the mushrooms in or they will go mushy and soggy, so cook them in several batches to ensure the pan stays hot. Discard any excess oil after frying.

Pour the remaining cream and lemon zest into a saucepan, set over a medium heat and bring to a simmer. Leave to cool for about 10 minutes.

Transfer the cooked field or button mushrooms, the cream, the rehydrated mushrooms and any liquor from the rehydrating into a food processor. Blend the mixture together until it is perfectly smooth. Taste and add ½ teaspoon of table salt to season and blend once more to combine.

Pour the mixture into the terrine dish or loaf pan, it should be almost firm at this point. Put in the fridge to firm up for at least 3 hours before serving.

Serve on a plate decorated with mixed pickled vegetables, a little mushroom ketchup and a few wedges of toast on the side. Use two spoons to make a quenelle of parfait and place on an endive or chicory leaf. Finish with a few slices of jalapeño pepper sprinkled over the top.

Wild mushroom tart

PREPARE: **5 MINUTES** COOK: **25 MINUTES** SERVES: **4**

Simple tarts using sliced bread instead of pastry to make the cases are delicious served for breakfast or as a light lunch.

8 thin slices bread

4 eggs

250 g/9 oz. mixed fresh wild mushrooms

80 g/1 cup grated Parmesan cheese

butter, for spreading and frying

table salt and freshly ground black pepper, to season

peppery mixed salad leaves, to serve

2 muffin pans, 1 greased

Preheat the oven to 180°C (350°F) Gas 4.

To make the tart cases, butter both sides of the slices of bread and remove the crusts. Place two pieces of bread in a muffin mould, set at a 45-degree angle from each other. Press the bread into the moulds then place the second muffin pan on top, holding the bread in place. Press the pans together using a weight (a heavy casserole dish or similar) then bake in the preheated oven for 10 minutes. Remove from the oven, take off the top muffin pan and let cool for 5 minutes.

Crack a whole egg into each cooled tart case and sprinkle a little black pepper over the top.

Bake the eggs in the cases, still in the muffin pan, for about 10 minutes until the egg whites are just cooked but the yolk is still runny. If you prefer hard-cooked yolks, cook for 20 minutes at 160°C (325°F) Gas 3.

While the eggs are cooking, in a hot pan over a high heat, quickly fry the mushrooms for a couple of minutes in butter and add a generous pinch of table salt.

Once the eggs are cooked to your liking, cover with a generous amount of cooked wild mushrooms and a sprinkling of Parmesan.

Return to the oven at 180°C (350°F) Gas 4 (remember to increase it if you have reduced the temperature) for 2 minutes to melt the cheese.

Remove and serve hot with a peppery mixed salad.

The best burger

PREPARE: **20 MINUTES** COOK: **25 MINUTES** SERVES: **4**

This burger will beat any meat burger in my opinion. My restaurant is known for its smoked mashed potatoes which we've had on the menu for the last six years and this burger recipe uses smoked potatoes to create the same fabulous depth of savoury flavour that brings all the elements of this exceptional burger together.

200 g/7 oz. Maris Piper or other floury potatoes, peeled and grated

2 tablespoons plain/all-purpose flour

1 teaspoon sea salt, plus extra to season

a pinch of freshly ground black pepper

200 g/1¾ sticks butter

100 ml/⅓ cup vegetable oil

4 large Portobello mushrooms, stems removed

2 large beefsteak tomatoes, sliced

250 g/9 oz. halloumi cheese, sliced

4 large soft white rolls (at least 15 cm/ 6 inches in diameter), sliced in half

100 g/3½ oz. Cheddar cheese, grated

1 cooked beetroot/beet, grated*

leaves of 1 little Gem/Bibb lettuce

white sugar, to season

Tomato Ketchup (page 160), to serve

Worcestershire or 'Shire' Sauce (page 159), to serve

*Note: when handling beetroot/beets, always oil your hands to stop discolouration

Form the grated potatoes into a rough ball and smoke using the method on page 21 for 5 minutes, until a hint of smoke colour can be seen on the potatoes. Put the smoked potato in a bowl and add the flour, sea salt and a good pinch of black pepper. Stir to combine the ingredients.

Form the smoked potato mixture into four equal patties, about the same diameter as the bread rolls. Ideally, they should be at least 5 mm/¼ inch thick.

In a large frying pan/skillet set over a medium heat, put the butter and vegetable oil and heat until sizzling. Carefully place the potato patties in the pan and cook until they are just golden. Turn and repeat on the other side. Remove from the pan and set aside. Save the fat for basting.

Lightly sprinkle the mushrooms with sea salt, gill-side up, and set aside.

Sprinkle the tomato slices with a little sea salt and sugar.

Preheat the barbecue/outdoor grill to 200°C (400°F) Gas 5. Place the tomatoes and mushrooms directly on the grill, baste the mushrooms in their cooking juices and cook gill-side down for a couple of minutes uncovered. Add the halloumi slices and potato patties and continue cooking for a few minutes until the tomatoes and cheese are starting to colour. Turn everything over to cook the other side.

Butter the bread rolls using the basting liquid and place, buttered-side down, on the grill.

Sprinkle the grated Cheddar on top of the mushrooms along with a little drizzle of Worcestershire or 'Shire' sauce over the top. Close the lid and cook for 5 minutes.

If you prefer to cook indoors, use a large frying pan/skillet with a lid and follow the method as above.

To assemble your burgers, put some grated beetroot/beet on the roll bases, followed by a mushroom with melted Cheddar, potato patty, a splash of ketchup, 2 lettuce leaves, halloumi and tomato slices, topped with the bun. Use a wooden skewer to secure it all together.

Mushroom toad-in-the-hole with onion gravy

PREPARE: **15 MINUTES** COOK: **40 MINUTES** SERVES: **4**

A vegetarian version of this classic family dish, usually made with pork sausages. This recipe is lighter to eat and, I believe, tastier, with the flavour of roasted mushrooms and onion gravy making a satisfying and warming meal.

100 g/³/₄ cup plain/all-purpose flour

2 eggs

60 ml/¹/₄ cup ice-cold water

100 ml/¹/₃ cup whole milk

6 Portobello mushrooms

vegetable oil, to drizzle

table salt and ground white pepper, to season

GRAVY

4 onions, thinly sliced

50 g/3¹/₂ tablespoons butter

50 g/3¹/₂ tablespoons plain/all-purpose flour

200 ml/³/₄ cup whole milk

a 25 x 30-cm/10 x 12-inch baking dish or 4 mini baking dishes, lined with baking parchment

To make the gravy, put the onions in a heavy-based saucepan with the butter and a generous pinch of table salt and cook over a low heat for 25–30 minutes, until they are just starting to turn a golden colour. Cover the onions with the flour and continue to cook, turning the onions constantly for a further 5 minutes. With the onions still on the heat, slowly add the milk, stirring the mixture until all of the milk has been combined into a thick gravy. Add some water if needed, to achieve the desired viscosity.

To make the batter, add the flour and a pinch of salt and pepper to a bowl. Make a well in the middle of the flour and break both eggs into it. Using a whisk, mix the eggs and flour together, starting slowly from the centre. Once the ingredients are mixed, gradually add the water, mixing to a thick paste. Finally, add the milk, whilst continually mixing with the whisk until the batter is smooth. Cover and chill in the fridge for 20 minutes.

Preheat the oven to 180°C (350°F) Gas 4.

Drizzle the mushrooms with oil and sprinkle with a dusting of salt and pepper. Place them, gill-side up, in the baking dish or dishes and bake in the preheated oven for 15–20 minutes, until they are just starting to turn golden.

Remove from the oven and turn the oven up to 200°C (400°F) Gas 5. Pour the batter over the mushrooms and return to the oven for a further 15–20 minutes, until the batter has risen and is golden brown and crispy on top.

Remove the toad-in-the-hole from the baking dish or dishes and take off the baking parchment. If whole slice into four pieces and serve hot with lashings of onion gravy.

Puffball steak, chips and béarnaise sauce

PREPARE: **1 HOUR** COOK: **15 MINUTES** SERVES: **4**

The top-selling dish in many restaurants will be steak, chips and béarnaise sauce; my recipe is more than just a vegetarian substitute. It may not be possible for everyone to get hold of a puffball mushroom, but do give it a try because they're more than the equal to any fillet steak in terms of flavour. Try using Portobello or wild mushrooms as a substitute for the puffball if you can't find one.

4 large potatoes

1 litre/quart groundnut oil

75 ml/5 tablespoons white wine vinegar

10–12 fresh tarragon leaves

250 g/2 sticks plus 1 tablespoon butter

4 egg yolks

1 puffball mushroom or 4 Portobello mushrooms

vegetable oil, to coat

table salt and freshly ground black pepper, to season

a thermometer

Wash and cut large chips out of the potatoes (I prefer them with the skin still on) and rinse them under cold water. Put the chips in a saucepan filled with salted, cold water, set over a medium–high heat and bring to a simmer. Simmer until the chips are just starting to become rough on the edges. Strain, then pat dry with paper towels. Chill in the fridge for at least 30 minutes.

Pour the groundnut oil into a clean saucepan and preheat it to a temperature of 130°C (266°F) over a medium heat. Carefully put the chips in the oil and cook for about 10 minutes, until slightly golden. Remove from the oil, drain on paper towels and chill in the fridge for another 30 minutes.

To make the béarnaise sauce, you will need a handheld electric blender and a jug/pitcher of about 300-ml/10-oz. capacity that is only slightly larger in diameter than the blade end. Put the vinegar, tarragon leaves and a pinch of black pepper into a small saucepan set over a medium heat. Heat to boiling point, then simmer until the volume has reduced by approximately half. Take the pan off the heat. Slowly melt the butter in a separate pan over a low heat. Pour the liquid butter, vinegar reduction (including the tarragon leaves), egg yolks and a pinch of salt into the jug/pitcher. Slowly, put the stick blender into the glass, capturing the yolks under the blade. Start with a couple of pulses of the blender, then while continuously blending, pull the stick blender slowly out of the jug/pitcher combining the butter and yolks to form the sauce. It really is that simple. The sauce will keep for about 45 minutes at room temperature.

When you are ready to serve, return the oil to a temperature of 190°C (374°F) and cook the chips for about 5 minutes, until deeply golden brown.

To make the puffball steaks, trim the puffball and carve 4 steaks from it about 2-cm/¾-inch thick. Save the rest of the puffball for making a soup or stock.

Preheat a grill pan over a medium heat.

Heavily oil the steaks with vegetable oil and season generously with table salt and black pepper, before placing them onto the hot grill pan to blacken them and cook through. Turn three times to create a crisscross pattern from the griddle on both sides.

Serve with chips and loads of béarnaise sauce.

Truffle rarebit

PREPARE: **10 MINUTES** COOK: **5 MINUTES** SERVES: **4**

This is my take on a Welsh rarebit (or 'rabbit', to use the original name). I use stout or ale to make the sauce because it adds a satisfying depth of flavour to the dish. A sprinkle of summer truffle takes this from being a great rarebit to something exceptional.

50 g/3½ tablespoons butter

50 g/3½ tablespoons plain/all-purpose flour

300 ml/1¼ cups stout or ale beer

2 teaspoons English mustard

200 g/2 cups grated strong Cheddar cheese

8 slices brown bread, lightly toasted

1 small summer truffle or black truffle

table salt, to season

TO SERVE

cherry tomatoes, chopped

rocket/arugula

Vinaigrette (page 171)

Begin by making a roux. Put the butter and flour in a dry saucepan and set over a medium heat until the mixture forms crumbs and is just starting to colour. Slowly, add the beer and whisk to combine into a smooth, thick paste. Add the mustard and Cheddar and continue to whisk until it has combined and is smooth. Take off the heat. You should have a thick cheesy paste.

Preheat a grill/broiler to high.

Arrange the toasted bread on a baking sheet, then spoon the cheese sauce over them. Place under the hot grill/broiler for 3–4 minutes, until they are starting to bubble and just blacken a little. Remove and rest for a few minutes, or you will burn yourself trying to eat molten cheese.

Finely grate the truffle over the rarebits according to taste and serve with a salad made from chopped cherry tomatoes and rocket/arugula, tossed together with a vinaigrette.

Truffled goat's cheese and red cabbage verrine

PREPARE: **10 MINUTES** COOK: **45 MINUTES** SERVES: **4**

Verrines look stunning on the table, so make a great dinner party dish. Make sure you buy sturdy glasses with a rolled lip, to take a spoon being used in them. You can prepare this dish well in advance, then it only takes 2 minutes to assemble and serve.

100 g/3½ oz. soft goat's cheese

50 ml/3½ tablespoons double/heavy cream

truffle oil, to taste

½ red cabbage, thinly sliced

200 ml/¾ cup red wine

30 g/2 tablespoons demerara/tubinado sugar

2 slices French loaf or ciabatta, sliced into 1-cm/³/8-inch cubes

olive oil, to coat

sea salt and freshly ground black pepper, to season

mustard cress shoots, to serve

In a small saucepan over a low heat, melt the goat's cheese and cream together. Take the pan off the heat and whisk to combine into a thick cream. Cool for 10 minutes, then whisk again to add some air into the mixture, then add a little truffle oil (use 1 level teaspoon of truffle oil to start, adding a little more depending on the strength of the oil).

Put the red cabbage in a heavy-based saucepan, along with the red wine, 200 ml/¾ cup of water and the sugar.

Bring to a low simmer over a medium heat and cook for 30–40 minutes until the liquid is reduced to a treacle-like consistency; stir occasionally to ensure all of the cabbage is cooked evenly.

Tip: When the liquid has reduced by two-thirds, pay close attention to the final cooking, as it will catch and burn the moment your back is turned!

Preheat the oven to 180°C (350°F) Gas 4.

While the red cabbage is cooking, make croutons from the bread. Put the cubes of bread into a large mixing bowl with plenty of olive oil and a generous amount of sea salt and black pepper, and toss together to evenly coat them. Spread onto a non-stick baking sheet and bake in the preheated oven for 8–10 minutes, until they are just starting to brown. Don't worry if the croutons are not totally crisp, they will crisp up as they cool down in the air.

Spoon the goat's cheese cream into four large, wide glasses and leave to cool in the fridge for at least 30 minutes. Transfer the cooled cabbage and croutons to the fridge, too, to cool everything down.

Once cooled, but for no more than 30 minutes before serving, spoon 2–3 tablespoons of the red cabbage mixture on top of the cream, then add the croutons. Finally, sprinkle some mustard cress over the top to finish and serve.

Cep omelette

PREPARE: **15 MINUTES** COOK: **25 MINUTES** SERVES: **4**

Fresh wild mushrooms are such a treat. This recipe is simple and makes the most of the ceps' wonderful flavour; sometimes I add a sprinkling of cheese on top or a hint of truffle oil to give it an even bigger punch. Only use wild mushrooms you are 100% sure are edible, otherwise use commercially grown varieties.

200 g/7 oz. cep mushrooms

a generous knob/pat of butter

1 onion, finely diced

leaves of 4 sprigs of fresh thyme

150 ml/²/₃ cup double/heavy cream

6 eggs

Tabasco sauce, to taste

table salt, to season

Firstly, prepare the mushrooms; use a paintbrush to dust off any grit or dirt, but do not wash them. Slice them into strips about 5 mm/¼ inch wide.

Preheat the oven to 160°C (325°F) Gas 3.

Put the butter and a pinch of table salt into a heavy-based ovenproof frying pan/skillet and melt over a medium heat. When the butter is sizzling, add the mushrooms, then the chopped onion and leave until the mushrooms start to turn golden. Do not stir the mushrooms or shake the pan, or they will go wet and mushy. Turn the mushrooms over, add the thyme leaves and take the pan off the heat.

In a large mixing bowl, quickly whisk together the cream, eggs, a few good glugs of Tabasco sauce and 1 teaspoon of table salt. Pour the mixture over the mushrooms and gently stir to combine everything evenly.

Put the pan in the oven for 15–20 minutes until the omelette/omelet has just set and is starting to turn golden on top. Place under a hot grill/broiler to finish cooking the top if necessary.

Portion and serve immediately.

Pappardelle Napolitana

PREPARE: **5 MINUTES** COOK: **45 MINUTES** SERVES: **4**

Pasta sauce Napoli-style but with added mushrooms and herbs is a winner! You can cook this well in advance and keep for a day or two in the fridge.

4 garlic cloves, crushed

250 g/9 oz. mixed mushrooms

1 onion, finely diced

150 g/$\frac{1}{2}$ cup concentrated tomato purée/paste

2 fresh bay leaves

3 sprigs of fresh thyme

600 ml/2$\frac{1}{2}$ cups vegetable stock

300 g/11 oz. bronze-dyed dried pappardelle pasta

extra virgin olive oil, for frying

table salt and freshly ground black pepper, to season

100 g/1$\frac{1}{2}$ cups grated Parmesan cheese, to serve

Just cover the base of a large saucepan with olive oil and set over a medium heat. Add the garlic, cleaned mushrooms and onion and cook for a few minutes until they start to colour. Add the tomato purée/paste, bay leaves and thyme and cook for 2–3 minutes. Slowly add the stock, stirring to combine. Leave the sauce to simmer and infuse for at least 30 minutes before making the pasta; add a little water if it starts to thicken too much.

Half fill a large saucepan with water and bring it to a rolling boil over a high heat. Add a 1–2 teaspoons of table salt, then the dried pasta. Leave on a rolling boil for 1 minute less than the amount of time the pasta instructions state to cook it for.

Once the pasta is cooked, drain, then immediately add to the pan with the sauce. Turn the pasta several times to coat it with sauce and remove the bay leaves and thyme sprigs.

Serve in bowls with a generous topping of Parmesan cheese and a good sprinkling of black pepper.

Chef's storecupboard

SAUCES • RELISHES • PICKLES • DRESSINGS

I loved writing this chapter, thes sauces and pickles taste amazing and are remarkably easy to make at home. Pickling and storing to extend the season of vegetables and fruits has been done since we learnt to grow and harvest, thousands of years ago.

For many, like me, the thought of crunching my way through a jar of Gran's indigestible home-pickled red cabbage is enough to bring me out in a cold sweat but things have changed and I hope you'll try my recipes and make them your own. It's easy to do and adds a wonderful acidic note to balance your dishes.

There's more than just pickling here, too. The Smoked Tomato Ketchup on page 160 is truly addictive. My 'Shire' Sauce on page 159 isn't meant to copy a classic Worcestershire Sauce but to be used in its place; it has similar flavours but is less acidic and more savoury. Try it with some plain rice and peas and you'll have a delicious and frugal meal. I've developed a taste for Kimchi, my recipe on page 167 is fairly mild. Try it and, if you like, you can boost the chilli/chile elements and leave it to pickle and ferment for longer than specified – some kimchi recipes call for 6–12 months to fully develop the flavours but I'd start with a lot less time first!

My recipes don't use preservatives, so keep a closer eye on storage dates than you would for a commercial sauce or preserved product, you can't expect them to last for months at the back of the fridge. Make them in small batches and share a few with friends as gifts.

Mayonnaise

PREPARE: **5 MINUTES** MAKES: **250 ML/9 OZ.**

This recipe works well with a good free-range chicken egg but I prefer to use duck eggs, as they add a level of complexity of flavour and creaminess as well as a deep yellow colour. Please note the egg is not cooked, so treat with caution for young children or pregnant ladies.

200 ml/¾ cup first-press rapeseed oil or light olive oil

15 ml/1 tablespoon white wine vinegar

1 teaspoon Dijon mustard

a pinch of table salt

1 duck egg

To make the mayonnaise, you will need a handheld electric blender and a jug/pitcher of about 300-ml/10-oz. capacity that is only slightly larger in diameter than the blade end.

Pour the oil, vinegar, mustard and a pinch of salt into the jug/pitcher, then crack the egg in.

Slowly place the blender into the jug/pitcher, capturing the yolk under the blender end. Start with a couple of pulses, then while continuously blending, pull the blender slowly up the jug/pitcher combining the oil and egg to form the mayonnaise, it really is that simple.

No-egg mayonnaise

PREPARE: **5 MINUTES** MAKES: **350 ML/13 OZ.**

This is a great mayonnaise for adding flavours to, as well as enjoying on its own; try mixing in some dill, garlic or even ketchup to make flavoured sauces. The recipe requires a few unusual ingredients but they are available at any good health food store or online, and are good storecupboard items with long shelf lives.

¼ teaspoon xanthan gum

a pinch of table salt

60 ml/¼ cup boiling water

1 teaspoon tapioca flour

4 teaspoons sherry vinegar

250 ml/1 cup first-press rapeseed oil

The method here is similar to traditional mayonnaise.

You will need a handheld electric blender and a jug/pitcher of about 300-ml/10-oz. capacity that is only slightly larger in diameter than the blade end.

Put the xanthan gum, salt, boiling water and tapioca flour in the jug/pitcher and process with the blender to form a silky smooth mixture.

With the blender on its fastest setting, add the vinegar, then start pouring the oil into the jug/pitcher; the oil will start to form a thick yellow mayonnaise. Keep pouring until all of the oil is in the cup, blending for 15–20 seconds in total, and the mayonnaise will be ready.

Chill in the fridge and use as necessary.

'Shire' sauce

PREPARE: **10 MINUTES** COOK: **1 HOUR (PLUS MATURING TIME OF 14 DAYS)** MAKES: **ABOUT 500 ML/18 OZ.**

This is my take on the classic Worcestershire sauce, a vegetarian version that is milder in heat. A couple of weeks spent infusing the flavours is needed to make this sauce come to its full potential.

100 ml/⅓ cup vegetable oil

2 onions, peeled and diced

400 g/2 cups canned chopped tomatoes

¼ teaspoon xanthan gum

50 g/¾ cup grated Parmesan cheese

50 g/2 oz. tamarind pulp

2 teaspoons dark miso paste

2 teaspoons table salt

8 cardamom pods

1 teaspoon each of ground cloves, freshly ground black pepper, ground cinnamon and cayenne powder

200 ml/generous ½ cup treacle or black strap molasses

300 ml/1¼ cups white wine vinegar

Put the vegetable oil and onions in a heavy-based pan and set over a medium heat. Cook until the onions just start to sizzle, then reduce the heat to low, cooking until they become glassy and have softened. Carefully add the tomatoes, xanthan gum, Parmesan, tamarind, miso, salt, cardamom, ground cloves, black pepper, cinnamon and cayenne powder. Increase the heat and cook until the mixture is bubbling. Leave on a very low simmer for 30 minutes then take off the heat.

Allow to cool for about 30 minutes, then add the treacle or molasses and the vinegar. Puree with a handheld electric blender or in a food processor. Push the finished mixture through a fine meshed sieve/strainer.

Pour into sterilized glass jars or bottles, seal and leave for a couple of weeks to allow the flavour to mature before using. With careful use of sterilized jars it will keep, sealed in a dark place, for months. Use within a few weeks once opened and store in the refrigerator.

Sweet chilli sauce

PREPARE: **2 MINUTES** COOK: **30 MINUTES** MAKES: **ABOUT 350 ML/13 OZ.**

This is a case of 'less is more'. The recipe uses ingredients you've probably already got in your storecupboard. When you use fresh ingredients, although they may limit the shelf-life, they produce a fresh, delicious and simple sauce. You'll never buy sweet chilli sauce again.

2 red Bird's eye chillies/chiles, thinly sliced diagonally

250 ml/1 cup white wine vinegar

250 g/1¼ cup white sugar

2 garlic cloves, crushed

Place the chillies/chiles, vinegar and sugar in a saucepan. Set over a medium heat, bring to a simmer and continue to simmer until the volume has reduced by half.

Remove the pan from the heat and leave to cool for about 5 minutes.

Add the garlic and stir to combine. Set aside for at least 15 minutes, to allow to cool and the flavours to infuse.

Use immediately or store in an airtight container in the fridge for up to 6 weeks. The mixture can become quite thick when it cools down, so do not store it in a bottle.

Note: The cooking of this sauce comes with a health warning. If you are tempted to speed-up the process by turning the heat up too high, the chillies/chiles and vinegar fumes are fierce, to say the least, so a low simmer and good ventilation are needed; you have been warned.

Do not be tempted to add the garlic any earlier than stated in the recipe. In boiling vinegar, garlic turns green; it still tastes good but nobody will want to eat it.

Tomato ketchup

PREPARE: **5 MINUTES** COOK: **15 MINUTES**
(PLUS INFUSING TIME OF 24 HOURS)
MAKES: **ABOUT 350 ML/13 OZ.**

Guilt-free ketchup! This is so simple to make and store but without the high salt and sugar content of commercial ketchup.

400 g/2 cups canned chopped tomatoes

2 teaspoons white sugar

1 teaspoon balsamic vinegar

a small pinch of dried ground
chillies/chiles

3 pitted black olives, finely chopped

grated zest of 1 lemon

1/2 level teaspoon xanthan gum

freshly squeezed juice of 1/2 lemon

Put all of the ingredients, except the lemon juice, in a heavy-based saucepan and set over a medium heat. Bring to a low simmer and continue to simmer for 10 minutes.

Add the lemon juice and purée using a handheld electric blender until smooth.

Pour through a fine mesh sieve/strainer into a sterilized glass jar or bottle. Seal and leave for at least 24 hours before using.

Once opened store in the fridge and use within 4 weeks.

Smoked tomato ketchup

PREPARE: **5 MINUTES** COOK: **45 MINUTES**
MAKES: **ABOUT 1 LITRE/QUART**

Tomatoes and smoke work extraordinarily well together. Adding a little smoke to food just seems to make everything taste better!

2 onions, quartered

1 kg/35 oz. ripe tomatoes

4 garlic cloves

50 ml/3 1/2 tablespoons vegetable oil

4–5 teaspoons balsamic vinegar

2 red (bell) peppers

2 teaspoons smoked paprika

1 teaspoon table salt

Preheat the oven to 180°C (350°F) Gas 4.

Put the onions on a baking sheet with the tomatoes and garlic. Drizzle with the vegetable oil and balsamic vinegar.

Roast in the preheated oven for 30–40 minutes. The tomatoes and onions should be starting to blacken, but not burnt, before you take them out of the oven.

Preheat a grill pan over a high heat and carefully place the (bell) peppers directly on the pan to blacken them.

Place the contents of the baking sheet, the blackened (bell) peppers and smoked paprika into a food processor and purée until smooth. Strain through a fine mesh sieve/strainer and the table salt. Spoon into a sterilized glass jar and seal.

Use generously on salads, in the Homemade Baked Beans recipe on page 112, on toasts with cheese grilled on top, or as a dipping sauce for chips. Amazing stuff!

Mushroom ketchup

PREPARE: **20 MINUTES** COOK: **45 MINUTES** (PLUS DRYING TIME) MAKES: **ABOUT 500 ML/18 OZ.**

The original ketchup was made using mushrooms, not tomatoes, and it makes a wonderful alternative to the ketchup we're used to. For me, it should taste of earthy mushrooms if used as a condiment, but I also use this to provide a savoury or 'umami' boost to dishes. This recipe makes a thick grainy paste.

500 g/18 oz. button mushrooms

100 g/3½ oz. dried mixed wild mushrooms

2 shallots

3 garlic cloves

40 g/scant ½ cup pitted black olives or anchovies

1 teaspoon table salt

125 ml/½ cup red wine

100 ml/⅓ cup ruby Port

1 tablespoon dark soy sauce

½ teaspoon powdered mace

1 teaspoon freshly ground black pepper

First, you need to dry the button mushrooms until they go wrinkly, like your fingers when you've been in the bath for too long. Preheat the oven to 60°C (125°F) Gas ¼. Put the mushrooms on a baking sheet and bake for 1 hour, or, if you don't have an oven that has a very low heat setting, leave uncovered on a sunny windowsill for 1–2 days.

Put the dried button and wild mushrooms in a food processor with the shallots, garlic, olives or anchovies. Pulse to combine.

Transfer the mixture to a heavy-based saucepan and set over a low heat. Add the salt and stir occasionally for 10 minutes. The mixture should have thickened slightly and darkened in colour.

Add the red wine, Port, soy sauce, mace and pepper, and stir to combine. Simmer, uncovered, for 20 minutes, stirring regularly.

Pour into a sterilized glass jar using a funnel. Seal and store in the fridge. Use within 2 weeks.

Beetroot ketchup

PREPARE: **20 MINUTES** COOK: **1 HOUR (PLUS RESTING TIME OF 1 WEEK)** MAKES: **ABOUT 1 LITRE/QUART**

Beetroot/beet is a chef's super-ingredient with a deep savoury flavour with sweetness and earthy tones... nothing like the horrible pickled beetroot/beets I had as a child.

500 g/18 oz. whole raw beetroot/beets

500 g/18 oz. parsnips, peeled and roughly chopped into 2-cm/¾-inch pieces

vegetable oil, to drizzle

50 ml/3½ tablespoons runny honey or agave syrup

50 g/3½ tablespoons white sugar

100 ml/⅓ cup white wine vinegar

table salt, to coat

Preheat the oven to 180°C (350°F) Gas 4.

Heavily salt then wrap the beetroots/beets in foil and put in the preheated oven to cook for 1 hour.

Spread the parsnip pieces out onto a baking sheet and drizzle with oil, honey and sugar, tossing them until they are just coated. Cook in the oven for 30 minutes.

Once cooked (check by prodding them with a sharp knife for any resistance), remove the beetroots/beets and parsnips. Take the foil and outer skin off the beetroots/beets and discard. The parsnips should be lightly browned.

Put the beetroots/beets, parsnips, sugar and vinegar in a food processor and purée until they form a smooth paste. Place a fine mesh sieve/strainer on top of a saucepan and press the purée through it, ensuring no hard lumps are left. Set over a medium heat and bring to a low simmer for 5 minutes, then pour the mixture into sterilized glass bottles and seal them.

Leave for at least 1 week before using. Use within 6 months of bottling.

Discard immediately if any mould is seen on the surface of the stored sauce as the pasteurization has failed.

Green tomato chutney

PREPARE: **20 MINUTES** COOK: **1½ HOURS** MAKES: **1.5 KG/3¼ LBS.**

If you grow your own tomatoes, there are always some green ones that just won't ripen. This recipe makes the most of their wonderful flavour and adds the sweetness they lack. Serve with mushrooms, eggs and brunch-style dishes.

600 g/21 oz. green tomatoes, trimmed and quartered

400 g/14 oz. ripe red tomatoes, trimmed and quartered, or 400 g/2 cups canned chopped tomatoes

200 g/7 oz. red onions, diced

1 small red chilli/chile, thinly sliced

4 garlic cloves, thinly sliced

250 ml/1 cup balsamic vinegar

250 ml/1 cup white wine vinegar

300 g/1½ cups white sugar

Put all of the ingredients into a large saucepan and set over a medium heat. Bring the mixture to a low simmer, then cover. Allow to simmer gently for 1 hour to cook everything thoroughly, stirring occasionally.

Take the lid off and turn up the heat to a rapid simmer and reduce the liquid until it is about one-third of the original quantity and has thickened to about the consistency of double/heavy cream.

Whilst hot, carefully spoon the chutney into sterilized glass jars ensuring even distribution of the liquid and solids. Seal the jars. As they cool, turn the jars over a few times to distribute the solids amongst the liquid. Store for up to 6 months and, once opened, store in the fridge and use within 4 weeks.

Chilli jam

PREPARE: **5 MINUTES** COOK: **15 MINUTES** MAKES: **350 ML/13 OZ.**

This is so simple to make and surprisingly delicious. Choose your chillies/chiles with caution, as the cooking will extract all of the heat from them... you have been warned. Use as a jam/jelly or an accompaniment to savoury dishes.

150 g/5 oz. red chillies/chiles, thinly sliced diagonally

6 tomatoes, deseeded and flesh finely chopped

500 ml/2 cups white wine vinegar

1 kg/35 oz. jam sugar

a sugar thermometer (optional)

Put the chillies/chiles (use as many or as few as you dare), tomatoes, vinegar and sugar in a heavy-based saucepan and set over a low–medium heat. Slowly bring to a rolling boil and keep at a rolling boil for about 10 minutes. If you have a sugar thermometer, check the temperature has reached 110°C (225°F) before removing the pan from the heat.

Leave to cool until the mixture is just starting to thicken and the chilli/chile slices stay suspended when you stir it.

Spoon carefully into sterilized glass jars. Seal and leave to finish cooling in the jars. Store for up to 6 months and, once opened, store in the fridge and use within 4 weeks.

Caramelized red onion chutney

PREPARE: **20 MINUTES** COOK: **2 HOURS** MAKES: **ABOUT 2 KG/4½ LBS.**

This chutney is a balance of sweet and sour flavours and the lovely depth you get from the red onions. I add a hint of heat and spice to really get your tastebuds working.

2 kg/4½ lbs. red onions

500 ml/2 cups balsamic vinegar

250 ml/1 cup sherry vinegar

200 ml/¾ cup red wine

500 g/18 oz. green apples, cored and diced into 5-mm/¼-inch cubes (skin on)

100 g/⅔ cup sultanas or golden raisins

150 g/¾ cup brown sugar

½ teaspoon ground cinnamon

1 teaspoon ground ginger

1 small red chilli/chile, thinly sliced

2 teaspoons table salt

Thinly slice the onions using a food processor. Chop them again using a knife, into thin, irregular pieces.

Put all of the ingredients in a large saucepan and set over a medium heat. Bring the mixture to a low simmer and cover. Allow it to simmer gently for 1½ hours, stirring occasionally, to cook everything thoroughly.

Take the lid off and turn up the heat to a rapid simmer. Reduce the liquid until it is about one-third of the previous quantity and has thickened to the consistency of double/heavy cream.

Spoon carefully into sterilized glass jars. Seal and leave to finish cooling in the jars. Store for up to 6 months and, once opened, store in the fridge and use within 4 weeks.

Piccalilli

PREPARE: **20 MINUTES** COOK: **1 HOUR 20 MINUTES** MAKES: **ABOUT 1 KG/2¼ LBS.**

Piccalilli works best on a cheese sandwich. This is my take on the classic English mustard and Indian spice chutney. I like the spices whole for the texture and the intense flavours that are released when they're eaten.

1 large cauliflower, cut into florets

300 g/11 oz. green beans, trimmed and chopped into short pieces

3 onions, finely chopped

1 celeriac/celery root, diced

2 fennel bulbs, diced

1 aubergine/eggplant, diced

1 red (bell) pepper, deseeded and diced

2 courgettes/zucchini, deseeded and diced

6 large green chillies/chiles, thinly sliced

100 g/1 cup sweetcorn/corn kernels

table salt, to taste

5 teaspoons cumin seeds

5 teaspoons coriander seeds

2 teaspoons mustard seeds

2 teaspoons ground cinnamon

4 teaspoons dried ground turmeric

4 garlic cloves, crushed

3 teaspoons cornflour/cornstarch

4 teaspoons English mustard powder

300 ml/1¼ cup cider vinegar

200 ml/¾ cup sherry vinegar

100 g/½ cup white sugar

Put all of the prepared vegetables and the sweetcorn/corn into a bowl of heavily salted cold water. Set aside for 1 hour.

In a deep, dry frying pan/skillet set over a medium heat, cook off the cumin, coriander and mustard seeds, cinnamon and turmeric until the seeds are just starting to pop. Take off the heat and add the crushed garlic, cornflour/cornstarch and mustard powder. The garlic will cook in the residual heat from the pan.

Slowly add the cider vinegar and return to the heat, continuously stirring to make a paste. Add the sherry vinegar and sugar and bring to a low simmer for 2 minutes.

Drain the vegetables of the cold salted water and add them to the hot mixture. Bring to a low simmer for 3–4 minutes, until the celeriac is just tender.

Take off the heat and carefully spoon the piccalilli into sterilized glass jars. Seal and leave for at least 1 week before using. Use within 2 weeks.

Vegetable pickles

PREPARE: **45 MINUTES**   COOK: **10 MINUTES**   MAKES: **ABOUT 2 KG/4½ LBS.**

Pickles are a restaurant staple of mine which inject colour and life into a plate. I have used two methods here, the first is to get the best from each vegetable with some additional herbs and chilli/chile spice to balance flavours, the second, combination method, is ideal if you want to make jars of mixed pickles for storage or gifts.

200 ml/¾ cup white wine vinegar

70 g/⅓ cup white sugar

1 small cauliflower, thinly sliced

1 cucumber

a bunch of fresh dill

2 carrots, cut into matchsticks

fresh tarragon leaves

1 red onion, sliced into rings

1 small hot chilli/chile

1 celery stick, sliced

1 celeriac/celery root, peeled and diced into 5-mm/¼-inch cubes

1 fennel bulb, thinly sliced across the bulb

freshly ground black pepper

1.5 litres/quarts white wine vinegar

dried whole green and red peppercorns (for combination method only)

Put the white wine vinegar and sugar in a saucepan with 200 ml/¾ cup of water and set over a medium heat. Bring to a simmer then set aside. This is your pickling liquid.

Prepare a separate container for each vegetable you plan to pickle.

To pickle cauliflower; pour the hot pickling liquid over the cauliflower slices to just cover and leave to cool, the cauliflower should be just cooked.

To pickle cucumber; peel the cucumber and remove the ends. Using the peeler, make long thin slivers of the white part for the length of the cucumber, discard the centre, add fresh dill to the container, mix together and pour over the hot pickling liquid. Leave to cool.

To pickle carrots; put them in a small saucepan of the pickling liquid and leave to simmer for 3 minutes, add fresh tarragon leaves before decanting into a container to finish cooking and cool.

To pickle red onion; put the onion and chilli/chile into a small saucepan of pickling liquid, simmer for 3 minutes before decanting into a container to finish cooking and cool.

To pickle celery; pour the hot pickling liquid over the celery slices to just cover and leave to cool. The celery should be just cooked.

To pickle celeriac/celery root; put the it into a small saucepan of the pickling liquid and leave to simmer for 5 minutes before decanting into a container to finish cooking and cool.

To pickle fennel; put it in a small saucepan of the pickling liquid with 2 teaspoons of black pepper and leave to simmer for 5 minutes before decanting into a container to finish cooking and cool.

Combination method: To make all the vegetables into one pickled side, prepare all the vegetables as per the above apart from the cucumber which you should slice across, making rounds about 3 mm/⅛ inch thick. Use none of the herbs, cracked pepper or chilli/chile. Put 1 litre/quart of white wine vinegar, 1 litre/quart of water and 250 g/1¼ cups white sugar into a large saucepan, set over a medium heat and bring to a simmer. Add the fennel and celeriac with 2 teaspoons each of the dried red and green peppercorns. After 2 minutes, add the red onion and carrots then after 3 more minutes add the remaining vegetables and remove from the heat. Allow to cool then decant carefully into sterilized glass jars.

Kimchi

PREPARE: **30 MINUTES (PLUS FERMENTING TIME OF 2 DAYS MINIMUM)** MAKES: **ABOUT 1.2 KG/2³/4 LBS.**

Kimchi is a Korean staple that is becoming more widespread in the West. Don't be put off by the initial aroma of the fermentation, the flavours are extraordinary.

1 Chinese or Napa cabbage, cut into 2.5-cm/1-inch squares

1 onion, roughly chopped

2 tablespoons chilli/hot red pepper flakes, plus extra to taste

30 g/4 tablespoons thinly sliced ginger

1 bulb garlic (8–10 cloves), peeled

100 g/³/4 cup cooked brown rice

50 g/3 tablespoons dark miso paste

100 g/3¹/2 oz. tamarind purée/paste

300 g/11 oz. daikon radishes, grated

300 g/11 oz. carrots, grated

6 spring onions/scallions, thinly sliced

table salt, to taste

boiled white rice and spring onions/scallions, to serve

Put the cabbage in a bowl of heavily salted water for 3 hours. Ensure the cabbage is covered in water by using a saucepan lid, that is slightly smaller in diameter than the bowl, to press down on the cabbage leaves.

In a food processor, blend the onion, chilli/hot red pepper flakes, ginger, garlic, rice, miso and tamarind into a paste. Add the drained cabbage leaves, radish, carrots and spring onions/scallions and mix together.

Plut everything in an airtight container at room temperature and set aside for at least 2 days.

Open and allow the fermentation gases to escape before tasting, add more salt or chilli/hot red pepper flakes to taste, if required.

You can store it in the fridge, in an airtight container, for up to 6 weeks.

Serve with boiled plain rice. Decorate with sliced spring onions/scallions on top – they add a lightness of flavour to the hot, salty flavours of the kimchi.

Pickled onions

PREPARE: **10 MINUTES** COOK: **5 MINUTES (PLUS RESTING TIME OF 1 WEEK)** MAKES: **ABOUT 1 KG/2¹/4 LBS.**

I'm often disappointed by pickled onions as they can be harshly vinegary and have very little onion flavour. This recipe adds heat from chillies/chiles, a mix of vinegars and some spice from coriander seeds to infuse flavour into the pickling liquor. The pickling liquor is quite fiery hot so use only one chilli/chile if you prefer less heat.

500 g/18 oz. small shallots

400 ml/1²/3 cups malt vinegar

100 ml/¹/3 cup white wine vinegar

200 g/1 cup white sugar

2 tablespoons black peppercorns

2 tablespoons red peppercorns

2 Bird's eye chillies/chiles, thinly sliced

2 tablespoons coriander seeds

Put the shallots in a large saucepan with the vinegars, 100 ml/¹/3 cup of water, the sugar and peppercorns.

Add the chillies/chiles and coriander seeds, and bring the mixture to a low simmer over a medium heat, then take off the heat immediately.

Pour the mixture into sterilized glass jars and leave for at least 1 week before using.

Pesto

PREPARE: **10 MINUTES** MAKES: **ABOUT 300 G/10 OZ.**

A good kitchen's secret ingredient is a pesto, this is one of the simplest ways to inject flavour into a dish. Use simply with pasta or try something unusual like mixing it with lightly salted popcorn for a delicious fun nibble, we often serve this in the restaurant as an amuse bouche.

TRADITIONAL

100 g/³/4 cup pine nuts

50 g/³/4 cup finely grated Parmesan cheese

50 g/2 oz. sheep's milk cheese (or strong Cheddar cheese)

2 garlic cloves

leaves from a large bunch of fresh basil

olive oil, to drizzzle

sea salt, to taste

WILD GARLIC

100 g/³/4 cup hazelnuts

50 g/³/4 cup finely grated Parmesan cheese

50 g/2 oz. strong Cheddar cheese

100 g/3¹/2 oz. wild garlic/ramps flowers

first-press rapeseed oil, to drizzle

grated zest of 1 lemon

freshly squeezed juice of ¹/2 lemon

sea salt, to taste

DILL AND LEMON

100 g/³/4 cup walnuts

100 g/3¹/2 oz. soft goat's cheese

1 garlic clove

a large bunch of fresh dill

first-press rapeseed oil, to drizzle

grated zest and freshly squeezed juice of 1 lemon

sea salt, to taste

KALE

100 g/³/4 cup cashew nuts

100 g/1¹/4 cup finely grated Parmesan cheese

2 garlic cloves

a large bunch of fresh kale, stalks removed

olive oil, to drizzle

sea salt, to taste

Put the nuts, a pinch of sea salt, the cheese and garlic (but not the wild garlic/ramps flowers) in a small food processor or pestle and mortar.

Pulse or grind to a smooth paste.

Add the leaves and any lemon zest and pulse or grind again until the mixture is combined and smooth.

Add any lemon juice and oil as required to blend together until a pesto is formed, it should have the consistency to hold together when it is pressed between spoons.

Store in the fridge and use within 1 week of making.

Flavoured oils

PREPARE: **15 MINUTES** MAKES: **250 ML/9 OZ.**

Have fun playing with flavour combinations but don't add too many ingredients to your oils, or too much of any one flavour, less is definitely more as the flavours intensify with time. Homemade oils are fun and simple to make but they are not safe to keep, so make and use them as needed and never, ever, keep them at room temperature. Treat them like any fresh product and refrigerate and use within 3 days.

250 ml/1 cup olive oil or first-press rapeseed oil

ONE OF THE FOLLOWING

1 Bird's eye chilli/chile

1 garlic clove

2 leaves or 12 flowers wild garlic/ramps

2 teaspoons fresh thyme leaves

2 teaspoons fresh rosemary leaves

4 sun-dried tomatoes

peel of 1 lemon

For each of the oils, put the oil and flavouring in a food processor and blitz for a few minutes. Leave in the fridge for a couple of hours to infuse fully then serve.

Use for cooking in place of regular oil to add flavours to a dish.

Vinaigrettes

PREPARE: **15 MINUTES** MAKES: **250–350 ML/9–12 OZ.**

Oil and vinegar mixed together with some great fresh produce can lift your cooking to a new level. Try these recipes and experiment with fun and tasty combinations. Homemade vinaigrettes are much safer for storing than flavoured oils as the vinegar prevents most bacteria from growing. However, I would still advise making and using them straight away, or within a few days.

GENERAL PURPOSE

250 ml/1 cup olive oil or first-press rapeseed oil

100 ml/1/3 cup white wine vinegar

1 tablespoon runny honey

2 teaspoons Dijon mustard

a pinch of table salt

RASPBERRY

250 ml/1 cup vegetable oil

50 ml/3 1/2 tablespoons white wine vinegar

50 ml/3 1/2 tablespoons balsamic vinegar

100 g/2/3 cup fresh raspberries

a pinch each of ground white pepper and table salt

HERBY

250 ml/1 cup olive oil or first-press rapeseed oil

100 ml/1/3 cup white wine vinegar

2 teaspoons herb leaves (thyme, rosemary, sage, basil)

a pinch of table salt

HOT ASIAN

250 ml/1 cup vegetable oil

50 ml/3 1/2 tablespoons white wine vinegar

grated zest and freshly squeezed juice of 1 lime

1 Bird's eye chilli/chile

Add all of the ingredients to a food processor and blitz for a couple of minutes. Rest for 1 hour to infuse the flavours, shake before serving.

Use the general purpose vinaigrette on salads, or try it on burgers for a spark of flavour.

Try the hot Asian vinaigrette on a cold noodle salad with some cooked prawns/shrimp, chicken or tofu.

The herby vinaigrette works really well with cold new potatoes or as a dip for breads.

For something different at a dinner party, try the raspberry vinaigrette as a topping for ice cream or other dessert.

Resources

UK

INGREDIENTS

Abel & Cole
www.abelandcole.co.uk
+44 (0) 20 8944 3780
Organic fruit and vegetable delivery throughout the UK.

The Chile Seed Company
www.chileseeds.co.uk
+44 (0) 1539 558 110
Seller of an extraordinary array of chilli/chile seeds.

Fine Food Specialist
www.finefoodspecialist.co.uk
+44 (0) 20 7627 2553
Online shop for quality produce and hard-to-find ingredients – a haven for the daring and curious cook.

Natoora
www.natoora.co.uk
+44 (0) 20 7627 1600
An online farmers' market. Fresh fruit, vegetables, cheeses and deli foods available for home delivery.

Sous Chef
www.souschef.co.uk
+ 44 (0) 20 7998 5066
Online resource for adventurous cooks, offering ingredients, equipment, tableware and gifts inspired by leading chefs and international cuisine.

Waitrose
www.waitrose.com
+ 44 (0) 1344 825 232
Supermarket, selling fresh, quality food and drink. Stores across the UK and stockists of a wide range of baking ingredients and other quality food products.

Whole Foods
www.wholefoodsmarket.com
+44 (0) 20 7368 6100
Shop for high-quality natural and organic foods, committed to sustainable agriculture.

KITCHEN EQUIPMENT

Amazon
www.amazon.co.uk
Useful online marketplace for hard-to-find ingredients and equipment.

Continental Chef Supplies
www.chefs.net
+44 (0) 808 1001 777
Suppliers of catering equipment and clothing.

John Lewis
www.johnlewis.com
+44 (0) 1698 545 454
UK department store stocking everything from clothing to kitchen equipment and appliances.

KitchenAid
www.kitchenaid.co.uk
+44 (0) 3444 990 101
Premium kitchen appliances including the iconic stand mixer. Available from all good homeware stores.

Lakeland Ltd
www.lakeland.co.uk
+44 (0) 1539 488 100
'The home of creative kitchenware' and stockists of a wide range of cooking equipment.

The Pampered Chef
www.pamperedchef.co.uk
+44 (0) 1344 823 600
Direct seller of innovative kitchen tools, available through a network of Pampered Chef Consultants throughout the UK, USA and Canada.

Steamer Trading Cookshop
www.steamer.co.uk
+44 (0) 1273 483 300
Sellers of domestic appliances and equipment.

Thermapen
www.thermapen.co.uk
An indispensable tool for measuring precise temperatures.

US

INGREDIENTS

Eataly
www.eataly.com
High-quality food store for fresh and storecupboard produce as well as kitchen equipment.

Kalustyan's
www.kalustyans.com
Online grocery store offering a huge range of dried chillies/chiles and spices.

Marx Foods
www.marxfoods.com
A commercial supplier with a good stock of fresh, dried and ground chillies/chiles as well as other fresh produce.

Trader Joe's
www.traderjoes.com
Food market with locations across the USA.

Whole Foods Market
www.wholefoodsmarket.com
+1 (844) 936 2273
Shop for high-quality natural and organic foods, committed to sustainable agriculture.

KITCHEN EQUIPMENT

Amazon
www.amazon.com
Useful online marketplace for hard-to-find ingredients and equipment.

Cooking.com®
www.cooking.com
Cookware, bakeware, food storage and tableware.

Cooks Dream
www.cooksdream.com
+1 (866) 285 2665
Explore the site for baking pans of all shapes and size, royal icing mix, food coloring, pastry bags and tips and other baking supplies.

The Cooks Kitchen
www.thecookskitchen.com
Huge range of kitchenware delivered anywhere in the world.

Crate & Barrel
www.crateandbarrel.com
+1 (630) 369 4464
US department store stocking everything from clothing to kitchen equipment, appliances and stationery.

La Cuisine: The Cook's Resource™
www.lacuisineus.com
+1 (703) 836 8925
For a wide variety of finest quality ingredients and cookware, explore the website of this independently owned cooking store.

The Pampered Chef
www.pamperedchef.com
+1 (630) 261 8900
Direct seller of innovative kitchen tools, available through a network of Pampered Chef Consultants throughout the UK, USA and Canada.

Sur La Table
www.surlatable.com
Cooking utensils and equipment.

Williams-Sonoma
www.williams-sonoma.com
Cooking utensils, equipment, fine linens and food stuffs.

World Spice
www.worldspice.com
Seattle's premier spice, herb and tea shop with a great online collection of whole or ground dried spices.

Index

Acknowledgments

My inspiration for many of the dishes in this book come from Jo Francis, who is sadly no longer with us. Jo walked into my restaurant kitchen one day with baskets of delicious things she had collected from the woodlands and fields around Dorset. Her regular visits from then on introduced me to the wonderful flavours of wild mushrooms and hedgerow produce. She wanted other people to share her delight at the wonderful natural world we lived in, this was so poignant when we found out she had a terminal cancer. I will always treasure thoughts of her patience at my attempts to recognize mushrooms on the too few walks we shared and her delight to be able to sit in the window of our little restaurant, overlooking the town square, eating a meal that used some of the wonderful produce she'd collected, she taught me that I didn't need to cook with meat to make a complete meal.

Thank you Amanda for recipe testing, helping with writing, editing and generally doing a large part of the work involved in this book, well over and above the duties you signed up to when we got married.

Thank you to Steve Painter for his wonderful photography and to Lucy McKelvie for the food styling, to Steph and Julia at Ryland Peters & Small for patient editing and cajoling of me – they bring this book to life.

The publisher would also like to thank Fine Food Specialist for supplying the puffball mushroom for the recipe on page 149.